Readers' Theater for Pri...

Contents

Introduction 3

Teacher Resources

Individual Fluency Record 5

Individual Drama Record 6

Sequencing Map 7

Summarizing the Play 8

Understanding the Characters 9

Understanding the Play 10

Unit 1: Helping Hands

Play 1: The Crab and the Stone

Teacher's Notes 11

Cover/Cast List 13

Play 14

What Do You Remember? 16

What's That Word? 17

Write Away! On the Move 18

Play 2: Community Helpers

Teacher's Notes 19

Cover/Cast List 21

Play 23

What Do You Remember? 28

What's That Word? 29

Write Away! Just the Job 30

Play 3: The Lion and the Mouse

Teacher's Notes 31

Cover/Cast List 33

Play 34

What Do You Remember? 38

What's That Word? 39

Write Away! Helping Out 40

Unit 2: All in the Family

Play 4: Goldilocks and the Three Bears

Teacher's Notes 41

Cover/Cast List 43

Play 44

What Do You Remember? 48

What's That Word? 49

The Three Bears' Porridge 50

Play 5: No Problem!

Teacher's Notes 51

Cover/Cast List 53

Play 54

What Do You Remember? 58

What's That Word? 59

Write Away! No Problem Cooking 60

Play 6: The Strongest One of All

Teacher's Notes 61

Cover 63

Cast List 64

Play 65

What Do You Remember? 68

What's That Word? 69

Write Away! The Strongest One

of All Contest 70

Unit 3: Looking Up

Play 7: Chicken Little

Teacher's Notes 71

Cover 73

Cast List 74

Play 75

What Do You Remember? 80

What's That Word? 81

Write Away! Dear Journal 82

Play 8: The Planets

Teacher's Notes 83

Cover/Cast List 85

Play 87

What Do You Remember? 90

What's That Word? 91

Write Away! Take a Trip 92

Play 9: The Clouds

Teacher's Notes 93

Cover/Cast List 95

Play 96

What Do You Remember? 99

What's That Word? 100

Write Away! Cloud Story 101

Write Away! Weather Safety 102

Contents

Unit 4: Food Fun

Play 10: The Gingerbread Boy

Teacher's Notes 103
Cover 105
Cast List 106
Play 107
What Do You Remember? 112
What's That Word? 113
Gingerbread Boy Cookies 114

Play 11: The Around the World Lunch

Teacher's Notes 115
Cover 117
Cast List 118
Play 119
What Do You Remember? 122
What's That Word? 123
Write Away! Lunch Bag Surprise 124

Play 12: A Sheep in the Peppers

Teacher's Notes 125
Cover/Cast List 127
Play 128
What Do You Remember? 130
What's That Word? 131
Write Away! Go Away, Sheep! 132

Props: Animals

Baby Bear 133
Mama Bear .133
Papa Bear 134
Bee 134
Chicken 135
Cow 135
Crab 136
Dog 136
Duck 137
Fish 137
Fox 138
Goose 138
Horse 139
Lion 139
Monkey 140
Boy Mouse .140
Girl Mouse .141
Mr. Mouse .141
Mrs. Mouse .142
Pig 142

Rooster 143
Sheep 143
Snake 144
Turkey 144
Turtle 145

Props: People

Goldilocks .145
Old Man 146
Old Woman 146
Puppet Face Parts
Ears, eyes, noses, mouths 147

Props: Things

Badge 148
Bag of Money 148
Bus 148
Chalkboard 149
Cloud 149

Food

Buñuelos 149
Ham and Cheese Submarine Sandwich . .149
Peanut Butter and Honey Sandwich 150
Plantains 150
Poori 150
Won Tons .150
Gingerbread Boy 151

Hose 151
Letters 151
Microphone 1 152
Microphone 2 152

Planets

Mercury 153
Venus 153
Earth 153
Mars 153
Jupiter 154
Saturn 155
Pluto 155
Uranus 156
Neptune 156

Statue 157
Stethoscope 157
Sun 157
Toothbrush .158
Wind 158

Answer Key 159

Readers' Theater for Primary Grades, SV 9309-2

Introduction

Overview

Readers' Theater for Primary Grades is a supplemental reading program designed to increase children's vocabulary, comprehension, and fluency. This collection of twelve plays will draw in even the most reluctant readers and help build their confidence through oral reading. The selections include well-known folktales, realistic stories, and nonfiction selections.

The National Reading Panel has identified fluency as one of the five basic areas of reading instruction. "Fluency is the ability to read a text accurately and quickly. Fluency is important because it frees students to understand what they read. Fluency can be developed by modeling fluent reading and by having students engage in repeated oral reading." (*Put Reading First*, p. 31)

Readers' theater is a way for students to practice orally rereading text by rehearsing and performing a play from a script that is rich in dialogue. "Readers' theater provides readers with a legitimate reason to reread text and to practice fluency. Readers' theater also promotes cooperative interaction with peers and makes the reading task appealing." (*Put Reading First*, p. 29)

A Variety of Reading Levels

Almost every child will be able to participate comfortably because of the wide range of reading levels found in the plays. Each play has four to eleven characters. Reading levels range from 1.1 to 3.9 as measured by the Spache and Dale-Chall readability formulas.

Teacher's Notes

Two pages of **Teacher's Notes** before each play provide easy-to-follow teaching suggestions.

Play Summary provides an overview of each play. You may use the summary to become familiar with the plot of the play quickly.

Meet the Players provides a list of characters and identifies the readability levels for each part.

The list may be used to assign appropriate parts based on children's reading levels.

Character Props suggests uses for the reproducible faces and symbols furnished in the Props section in the back of the book. This section also lists each prop and the page number on which it can be found. Please note that the emphasis of readers' theater is on fluency and comprehension rather than the prop product. The faces and symbols are used as icons in the play script to identify each speaker for added interest.

Play Props is a list of possible backgrounds and minor implements that could be used to present the play.

Tapping Prior Knowledge prepares and motivates children to read the play. Several questions are provided that elicit personal responses from children—based on individual experiences and feelings.

Vocabulary lists six to ten words in the play that children might find difficult to understand or read. According to current research, familiarity with vocabulary is a prerequisite for fluency. Therefore, emphasize these words in vocabulary exercises before children read a play. English language learners may need special attention.

Fluency targets a specific verbal skill in each play. Suggestions explain where to find the example, how to model it, and ways to practice the word, phrase, or sentence to develop fluency.

Comprehension identifies a comprehension skill pertinent to many standards for the early elementary child and lists suggestions to help guide children as they explore the skill.

Extending the Play provides ideas for cross-curricular activities, including language arts, social studies, science, and writing. The activities may be used to enrich the children's reading of the play individually or in small or large groups.

Comprehension Activities

Three comprehension activities follow each play.

What Do You Remember? explores children's understanding of main idea, details, sequence, drawing conclusions, and context in a test

Readers' Theater for Primary Grades, SV 9309-2

format. An open-ended, short-answer writing question concludes this page.

What's That Word? is a vocabulary enrichment page. A variety of exercises reinforce the difficult vocabulary words in each play.

Write Away! requires children to combine a readers' theater experience with composition skills. The exercises are designed to elicit both analytical and creative responses to the ideas explored in the play.

Teacher Resources

Individual Fluency Record is a chart that lists specific fluency skills children should exhibit when reading out loud. You may wish to note each child's strengths and weaknesses as he or she reads a play part and maintain a record to chart each child's progress throughout the year.

Individual Drama Record provides a general observation of individual children as they work in the group to perform the play.

Sequencing Map is a means by which children track the events in a play.

Summarizing the Play is a page that children make into a booklet that highlights the important parts of the play.

Understanding the Characters encourages children to describe characters based on looks, personality, and actions.

Understanding the Play asks questions about the elements of the play, including characters, setting, and plot.

Props are large reproducibles that children can use to enhance their parts in the play and help the audience know who is reading. They are listed alphabetically in the categories of animals, people, and things.

Props

A large variety of animal faces, people faces, facial features, community helper tools, and planet illustrations are found on pages 133 through 158. They can be reproduced to provide a wealth of fun and creative props for readers' theater participants. The props can be copied in relative size, reduced, or enlarged to accommodate your play needs. Keep in mind that readers' theater is a process that encourages the development of fluency and comprehension. The props are to be used as an avenue to help

maintain interest and audience understanding. The following are some creative prop ideas to enhance the reader's theater experience.

Headbands. Reproduced at the same size, the faces can be attached to a sentence strip to form a headband that performers wear. Young children can simply color the faces. More advanced children can use the props as patterns to cut out the parts from construction paper.

Puppets. Depending on the size of the reproducible props, children can make any number of puppets to hold as they read. They can make small and large paper-bag puppets, paper-cup puppets, and puppets on ice cream sticks.

Masks. Children can use paper plates and stapled rubber bands for earpieces to make character masks to be worn while reading. The prop illustrations can be applied directly to the paper plate or used as a pattern for the mask.

Necklaces. Children can color the props and thread them onto yarn or string to make necklaces to wear. You may wish to laminate the props if used in this way.

Vests. Help children cut a large grocery sack to make a vest. They can decorate the vest to match their part. The prop copy can be affixed to the vest as a badge emblem.

Badges. Children can simply color the prop and tape or paper clip the picture to their clothing.

Name _____ Date _____

Individual Fluency Record

	Needs Improvement	Satisfactory	Excellent
Expression			
Uses correct intonation for statements			
Uses correct intonation for questions			
Uses correct intonation for commands			
Uses correct intonation for exclamations			
Interjects character's emotions and moods			
Reads words in all capitals to express character's emotions			
Reads words in dark print to express character's emotions			
Reads onomatopoeia words to mimic character			
Volume			
Uses appropriate loudness			
Voice reflects tone of character			
Voice reflects feelings of character			
Speed			
Reads sentences smoothly with line breaks			
Reads words in short sentences as meaningful units			
Reads phrases and clauses as meaningful units			
Reads rhyming text at a constant speed			
Reads rhythmic text with a constant beat			
Punctuation			
Pauses at the end of sentences			
Pauses at commas that follow an introductory phrase			
Pauses at commas in a series			
Pauses at commas in a clause			
Pauses at commas after introductory names			
Pauses at ellipses			
Pauses at dashes			
Recognizes that question marks are questions			
Recognizes that exclamation points indicate strong feeling			
General			
Demonstrates confidence			
Feels at ease in front of an audience			
Speaks without being prompted			
Speaks at the appropriate time for the character's part			
Demonstrates the character's personality			

Teacher Comments _____

_____

_____

_____

Name _____ Date _____

Individual Drama Record

	Needs Improvement		Satisfactory		Excellent
1. Cooperates in the group task	1	2	3	4	5
2. Participates in class discussion	1	2	3	4	5
3. Combines personal experience with knowledge of stories when creating performance	1	2	3	4	5
4. Creates believable dialogue	1	2	3	4	5
5. Uses voice and intonation to communicate personality of character	1	2	3	4	5
6. Creates accompanying character prop	1	2	3	4	5
Overall Score	1	2	3	4	5

Teacher Comments _____

_____

_____

_____

_____

_____

_____

_____

_____

_____

_____

Readers' Theater for Primary Grades, SV 9309-2

Name _____ Date _____

Sequencing Map

 Write the title of the play. Then write or draw to tell what happens in the play.

Title _____

Beginning

[ ]

Middle

[ ]

End

[ ]

Summarizing the Play

⭐ **Cut out on the dotted lines. Fold along the solid lines to make a book. Write the title of the play. Then write or draw the answers to the questions.**

3

fold

2

fold What is the problem?

Who is in the play?

How is the problem solved?

Name

_____

Play Title

_____

_____

4

1

Name _____   Date _____

Understanding the Characters

 Choose a character from the play. Write the name. Write or draw to tell how the character looks and acts.

Character's Name

_____

How the Character Looks

_____

_____

_____

_____

How the Character Acts

_____

_____

_____

_____

Name _____   Date _____

Understanding the Play

 A play is a story that people act out. Every play has characters, a setting, and a problem that gets solved. Answer the questions to tell about the play.

The **title** is the name of the play.

1. What is the title of the play?

_____

The **characters** are the people or animals in the play.

2. What is the name of the most important character?

_____

3. What are the names of the other characters?

_____

The **setting** is where and when the play takes place.

4. Where does the play take place?

_____

5. When does the play take place?

_____

The **problem** is what the character must solve.

6. What problem does the character have to solve?

_____

7. What does the character do to solve the problem?

_____

8. How is the problem solved at the end of the play?

_____

The Crab and the Stone

Play Summary

Crab has a new home along the shore and finds the perfect stone to put near the opening of the hole. Because the stone is so large, Crab's friends offer to help. Fish pulls down when he dives. Duck pulls up when she flies. Crab pulls sidewise towards his home. As a result, the stone does not move anywhere. When Turtle comes along, he explains that the stone does not move because the friends are pushing and pulling in opposite directions. The friends then work together to move the stone.

Meet the Players

Character	Reading Level
Narrator	1.9
Crab	1.6
Fish	1.3
Duck	1.6
Turtle	2.0

Character Props

Children can use the following resources found in the back of the book to make headbands, armbands, puppets, or paper-plate masks.
Narrator: microphone 1, p. 152
Crab, p. 136
Fish, p. 137
Duck, p. 137
Turtle, p. 145

Play Props

You may wish to gather the following simple props for children to use during the play.
Ball
Large table (Children can position themselves above, under, and to the side of the table.)

Teacher's Notes

Research Base

"Readers' theater provides readers with a legitimate reason to reread text and to practice fluency." (*Put Reading First*, p. 29)

www.harcourtschoolsupply.com
11
The Crab and the Stone
Readers' Theater for Primary Grades, SV 9309-2

The Crab and the Stone

Tapping Prior Knowledge

Before reading the play, discuss these questions with children.

1. Think about the game tug-of-war. What happens when both teams pull?

2. Suppose you and a friend are trying to move a heavy box. What would happen if each of you were on opposite sides pulling?

3. What would be the best way to move the box?

Vocabulary

You may wish to introduce these words prior to reading the play. Children also can practice the words using the activity master on page 17.

shore, p. 14   *kind*, p. 14
large, p. 14   *string*, p. 14
stone, p. 14   *stuck*, p. 15

Fluency: Reading Rhythmic Text

The Crab and the Stone offers many opportunities for children to practice reading rhythmic text. Invite children to clap their hands to keep a steady beat. Then model how to read the text rhythmically. Pair children and have partners take turns clapping the beat and reading the text.

Comprehension: Recognizing the Main Idea and Supporting Details

After reading the play, draw a T-chart with the headings *Main Idea* and *Details*. Ask children: *What is this play mostly about? What are some details that helped you understand the story?* Record their responses under the appropriate heading.

Extending the Play

Use these activities to enrich the children's experience with readers' theater. The activities can be completed individually, in small groups, or as a shared writing experience.

1. Have children complete any or all of the activity masters on pages 7 through 10.

2. Invite children to retell the story in a narrative format from the point of view of the crab.

3. Reread Crab's couplet: *Thank you, friends, for my new door./I'll be safe along the shore.* Challenge children to write their own rhyming couplet using the beginning sentence frame: *Thank you, friends, for my new _____.*

4. Lead children in a discussion of animals and plants that live along a shore. Then invite partners to create dioramas of a shore environment using shoeboxes and art supplies.

Readers' Theater

FOR PRIMARY GRADES

Presents

The Crab and the Stone

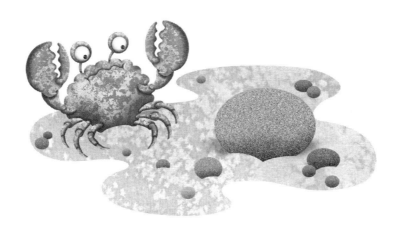

Cast
(in order of appearance)

Narrator _____

Crab _____

Fish _____

Duck _____

Turtle _____

www.harcourtschoolsupply.com
13
The Crab and the Stone
Readers' Theater for Primary Grades, SV 9309-2

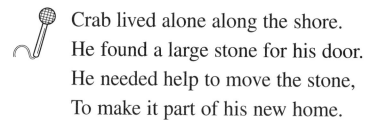
Crab lived alone along the shore.
He found a large stone for his door.
He needed help to move the stone,
To make it part of his new home.

Do you see that large, white stone?
I want that big stone for my home.

Hello, friend!
I will help you with that stone.
I will help you bring it home.

Thank you, Fish, you are so kind.
That is what I had in mind.

Fish tied a string around the stone
To help Crab bring that large stone home.

Push, pull, push, pull, push, pull.

Hello, friends!
I will help you with that stone.
I will help you bring it home.

Thank you, Duck, you are so kind.
That is what we had in mind.

Duck tied a string around the stone
To help Crab bring that large stone home.

Readers' Theater for Primary Grades, SV 9309-2

Push, pull, push, pull, push, pull.

Hello, friends!
I will help you with that stone.
I will help you bring it home.

We can try to pull once more.
Isn't that what friends are for?

Before you pull, please think with care,
Why this stone is still stuck here.
Duck pulls UP whenever she flies.
And fish pulls DOWN whenever he dives.
Then Crab is pulling TO his home.
You will never move that stone.

Oh, yes! We see just what you say.
Thank you, Turtle! You saved the day.

Crab and Duck pulled toward the shore,
While Turtle and Fish pushed it some more.
Soon the stone was at Crab's door.
The friends did not push anymore.

Thank you, friends, for my new door.
I'll be safe along the shore.

We used our brains and thought it out.
It did the trick, there is no doubt!

Name _____   Date _____

What Do You Remember?

 Darken the letter by the correct answer. Then answer the last question.

1. Why did Crab want the stone?

   Ⓐ to make a door

   Ⓑ to make a chair

   Ⓒ to make a table

2. What did the animals use to move the stone?

   Ⓐ a stick

   Ⓑ a string

   Ⓒ a store

3. Which way did Duck move the stone?

   Ⓐ to the side

   Ⓑ down

   Ⓒ up

4. Why didn't the stone move at first?

   Ⓐ It was stuck in the mud.

   Ⓑ The animals did not work together.

   Ⓒ The animals did not push hard enough.

5. Which animal found out why the stone did not move?

   Ⓐ Turtle

   Ⓑ Duck

   Ⓒ Fish

6. What is this story mostly about?

   _____

   _____

The Crab and the Stone
Readers' Theater for Primary Grades, SV 9309-2

What's That Word?

 Read the word in each puzzle. Find a word in the box that means the same. Write the word to complete the puzzle.

kind	large	stone	string	shore

1.

```
        r
        o
        p
        e
```

2.

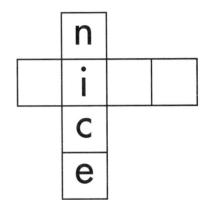
```
  n
  i
  c
  e
```

3.

```
  b
  i
  g
```

4.

```
  r
  o
  c
  k
```

5.

```
  b
  e
  a
  c
  h
```

Name _____   Date _____

Write Away! On the Move

Suppose you need to move a heavy box from your front door to your bedroom. How would you move it? Write a plan. Then draw a picture to go along with your plan.

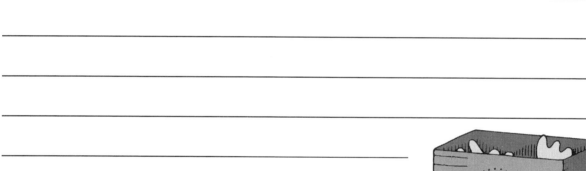

The Crab and the Stone
Readers' Theater for Primary Grades, SV 9309-2

Community Helpers

Play Summary

Using a game format, children read clues about nine community helpers: police officer, firefighter, mail carrier, doctor, dentist, store clerk, teacher, bus driver, and baker. The helper's name is identified after the clues are shared.

Meet the Players

Character	Reading Level
Narrator	2.8
Game-show host	1.9
Police officer	2.0
Firefighter	1.9
Mail carrier	2.7
Doctor	3.0
Dentist	2.6
Teacher	2.3
Store clerk	2.0
Bus driver	2.0
Baker	3.2

Character Props

Children can use the following resources found in the back of the book to make badges for grocery-sack vests, necklaces, armbands, or paper-bag puppets.

Narrator: microphone 1, p. 152
Game-show host: microphone 2, p. 152
Police officer: badge, p. 148
Firefighter: hose, p. 151
Mail carrier: letters, p. 151
Doctor: stethoscope, p. 157
Dentist: toothbrush, p. 158
Teacher: chalkboard, p. 149
Store clerk: bag of money, p. 148
Bus driver: bus, p. 148
Baker: gingerbread boy, p. 151

Teacher's Notes

Play Props

You may wish to gather the following simple props for children to use during the play.
Pre-recorded applause

Readers' Theater for Primary Grades, SV 9309-2

Community Helpers

Tapping Prior Knowledge

Before reading the play, discuss these questions with children.

1. What is a community?

2. Who are some people in our community that we call if we need help?

3. What are other kinds of jobs that people do in our community to help one another?

Vocabulary

You may wish to introduce these words prior to reading the play. Children also can practice the words using the activity master on page 29.

badge, p. 23   *hose*, p. 23   *cough*, p. 24   *chalk*, p. 25   *dough*, p. 27
uniform, p. 23   *address*, p. 24   *teeth*, p. 25   *price*, p. 26   *protect*, p. 27

Fluency: Reading Rhyming Text

Community Helpers offers many opportunities for children to practice reading rhyming text. Turn to page 24 and read the passage about a mail carrier. Help children notice words that rhyme. Point out the rhyming pattern. Next, point out that rhyming words may have different spelling patterns (*you/do*). Invite partners to choose a favorite community helper and rehearse the passage to develop fluency.

Comprehension: Drawing Conclusions

Explain that children can make good guesses if they know facts. Then choose one of the community helpers and read the passage aloud. After children name the helper, have them identify the words and phrases that helped them draw their conclusions.

Extending the Play

Use these activities to enrich the children's experience with readers' theater. The activities can be completed individually, in small groups, or as a shared writing experience.

1. Have children complete any or all of the activity masters on pages 7 through 10.

2. Challenge children to identify other community helpers. Write all the responses on the board. Then have them write four clues about one helper without using the name. Invite children to share their riddles with the class.

3. Point out that the school has many community helpers. Ask children to choose one school helper, draw a picture of that person, and write a sentence about the job the helper does. Hang the work in the hallway with the title "Hall of Helpers."

Readers' Theater

FOR PRIMARY GRADES

Presents

Community Helpers

Cast
(in order of appearance)

Narrator _____

Police Officer _____

Game-Show Host _____

Firefighter _____

Readers' Theater

FOR PRIMARY GRADES

Cast
(in order of appearance)

Mail Carrier _____

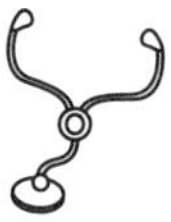

Doctor _____

Dentist _____

Teacher _____

Store Clerk _____

Bus Driver _____

Baker _____

Readers' Theater for Primary Grades, SV 9309-2

There are people in our town.
We see them every day.
They have special jobs to do.
They help in many ways.
We would like for you to play
A community helper game.
We will give you several clues.
Then you guess the helper's name.

I make sure you follow laws.
I keep you safe and sound.
You might see me in a car,
Or walking around town.
I wear a badge and radio.
I wear a uniform, too.
I write facts in a notebook.
I'm a friend to you.

Who is this helper? Do you know?
If you said, "police officer," way to go!

Clang, clang! I hear the bell.
I slide right down the pole.
I grab my hat, my boots, and coat.
I jump in the truck and go.
I race to a house that's burning fast.
I get my ladder and hose.
Then I spray water on the house.
And out that fire goes!

 Who is this helper? Do you know?
If you said, "firefighter," way to go!

 I read the zip code and address.
I read the person's name.
I'm sure these letters belong here.
The mailbox says the same.
I bring you cards and letters
That people mail to you.
I also pick up things you send,
Because that's the job I do.

 Who is this helper? Do you know?
If you said, "mail carrier," way to go!

 You visit me when you are well,
But mostly when you're ill.
You cough, and sneeze, and blow your nose.
You might have caught a chill.
I listen with a stethoscope.
I look inside your ear.
Sometimes I give you medicine
To help the sickness clear.

 Who is this helper? Do you know?
If you said, "doctor," way to go!

You need your teeth to help you eat.
They bite, and crunch, and chew.
I'm the one that keeps teeth strong
And makes them white for you.
I show you how to brush your teeth
And floss them in between.
You'll keep your teeth a long, long time,
If you keep them clean.

Who is this helper? Do you know?
If you said, "dentist," way to go!

I teach you how to read and think.
I teach you how to write.
I teach you math and science skills.
I give you work at night.
Chalk and pencils are some tools
That we use every day.
But anytime you come to school,
We have fun in work or play.

Who is this helper? Do you know?
If you said, "teacher," way to go!

Page 4

Stop and look at what I sell,
Clothes, and food, and more.
I will help you find something
When you're in my store.
Choose the thing you want to buy.
Then look at the price tag.
Pay with money that you have.
I'll put it in a bag.

Who is this helper? Do you know?
If you said, "store clerk," way to go!

If you want to go someplace,
I will take you there.
Watch the time and wait for me.
You'll have to pay a fare.
Climb on board and find a seat.
I drive along the road.
Pull a string, and I will stop.
And then you can unload.

Who is this helper? Do you know?
If you said, "bus driver," way to go!

If you're hungry, come see me.
I sell tasty treats.
Fresh baked cookies, cakes, and pies
Are things you like to eat.
Early every morning,
I mix up lots of dough.
I bake it in large ovens.
You buy these treats to go.

Who is this helper? Do you know?
If you said, "baker," way to go!

The helpers here are just a few
From our community.
There's not the time to talk about
All the others that we see.
There are bankers, builders, lawyers,
And truckers, to name a few.
We can't forget the service people
Who protect our freedom, too!
We are thankful to these helpers
For the special jobs they do.
They make the town a better place
Just for me and you.

Name _____   Date _____

What Do You Remember?

 Darken the letter by the correct answer. Then answer the last question.

1. What would a doctor use?

    Ⓐ some chalk

    Ⓑ a hose

    Ⓒ a stethoscope

2. What does a firefighter do?

    Ⓐ put out fires

    Ⓑ teach children to read

    Ⓒ sell things

3. Which of the things below would a mail carrier **not** bring to you?

    Ⓐ a cough

    Ⓑ a letter

    Ⓒ a card

4. Who works in a school?

    Ⓐ a firefighter

    Ⓑ a teacher

    Ⓒ a game-show host

5. Who helps you buy things?

    Ⓐ a police officer

    Ⓑ a bus driver

    Ⓒ a store clerk

6. Why is it important to have many different helpers in a community?

    _____

    _____

Name _____ Date _____

What's That Word?

 Write a word from the box to label each picture.

address	badge	chalk	cough	dough
hose	price	protect	teeth	uniform

1.

_____

2.

_____

3.

_____

4.

_____

5.

_____

6.

_____

7.

_____

8.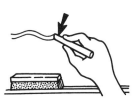

_____

9.

_____

10.

_____

Name _____   Date _____

Write Away! Just the Job

⭐ **Which community helper job would you like to do? Write sentences telling why you like this job. Then draw a picture to show what you would look like if you were this helper.**

_____

_____

_____

_____

_____

_____

The Lion and the Mouse

Play Summary

A lion catches a mouse that has mistakenly run up on its back. The mouse, promising to help the lion someday, asks the lion to let it go. The lion releases the little mouse, not expecting help in return. After all, the mouse is so little, and the lion is king of the jungle. Soon, the lion is caught in a net. The mouse comes to the lion's rescue when it uses its teeth to cut through the ropes.

Meet the Players

Character	Reading Level
Narrator	2.0
Lion	1.8
Monkey	2.6
Snake	1.1
Mouse	1.3

Character Props

Children can use the following resources found in the back of the book to make headbands, paper-plate masks, necklaces, armbands, or paper-bag puppets.
Narrator: microphone 1, p. 152
Lion, p. 139
Monkey, p. 140
Snake, p. 144
Mouse, p. 140

Play Props

You may wish to gather the following simple props for children to use during the play.
Jungle trees cut from green and brown mural paper
Cloth (for net)

Research Base

"Readers' theater [is] a holistic method suitable for building fluency, sight word knowledge, and interest."
(Rinehart, p. 75)

The Lion and the Mouse

Tapping Prior Knowledge

Before reading the play, discuss these questions with children.

1. What are some ways that you help others?

2. Have you ever helped someone who was bigger and stronger than you? How did you feel?

3. Suppose someone needed help. What are some reasons that you would not help the person?

Vocabulary

You may wish to introduce these words prior to reading the play. Children also can practice the words using the activity master on page 39.

jungle, p. 34	*sharp*, p. 36
trouble, p. 34	*gnawed*, p. 36
roared, p. 36	*cheered*, p. 37

Fluency: Interjecting Feeling and Characterization

The Lion and the Mouse offers many opportunities for children to practice interjecting feeling and characterization. As children read their parts, point out that an exclamation point signals strong feeling. Discuss how the character might be feeling at that point in the story and that children should use their voice to match that feeling.

Comprehension: Understanding Cause and Effect

Model a cause and effect statement: *The lion was trapped so he roared*. Record the information in a T-chart under the headings *Cause* and *Effect*. Invite children to page through the text to find other examples of cause and effect situations. Write the responses in the chart.

Extending the Play

Use the activities to enrich the children's experience with readers' theater. The activities can be completed individually, in small groups, or as a shared writing experience.

1. Have children complete any or all of the activity masters on pages 7 through 10.

2. Ask children to pretend to be the lion in the story. Have them write a thank-you note to the mouse.

3. Help children compile a list that identifies the characteristics of a good friend.

Readers' Theater
FOR PRIMARY GRADES

Presents
The Lion and the Mouse

Cast
(in order of appearance)

Narrator _____

Lion _____

Monkey _____

Snake _____

Mouse _____

 **Page 1**

 One day, a lion lay asleep in the jungle. A mouse did not watch where it was going. The mouse ran up the lion's tail and right onto its back. The lion awoke and down came its huge paw over the mouse.

 Look what I caught! Lunch!

 The other animals in the jungle did not want to help.

 Oh, oh! Mouse is in big trouble. I won't go help. Lion will catch me if I do.

 Poor Mouse! There is nothing that I can do. Lion has such strong paws! He will catch me, too.

 The little mouse began to shake as it begged the lion to be set free.

 Please, Lion. Let me go. If you do, I'll come back and help you someday.

 Ha, ha, ha! How could you ever do anything to help me? You are so tiny!

34

The Lion and the Mouse
Readers' Theater for Primary Grades, SV 9309-2

 I will find a way!

 Well, you really aren't much of a meal anyway. So, I guess I will let you go.

 The lion put down the little mouse. Quickly it ran away into the tall grass.

 Wow! Mouse is very lucky.

 Yes! I think Mouse will stay far away from Lion now.

 Later that day, the lion was walking through the jungle. The lion got trapped in a hunter's net.

 Help! Help! I am trapped in a net! Someone please come help me!

 The monkey and snake looked down from their places high in the trees.

 I can't help! I still think you will eat me.

 I think Monkey is right. I can't help you either.

The unhappy lion roared and roared. Soon, the little mouse heard the lion's cries. It ran through the grass to the lion.

Here I am, Lion! I can help you. I will help you get out of the net.

You cannot help me, Mouse! You are very little, and I am trapped in this net. The net is tied to the branch of this tree.

Oh, yes, I can help! I have sharp teeth for biting. I can climb trees, too. I will climb the tree and bite through the rope of the net.

Please hurry, Mouse! The hunter will come back soon!

The mouse quickly climbed up the tree. It gnawed on the rope until the rope broke. The lion fell to the ground.

I am free! I am free! Thank you, Mouse.

Was I not right? Did I find a way to help you?

 Yes, Mouse! You were right. You did help me, even though I am so big, and you are so little.

 All the animals in the jungle cheered for the little mouse.

 Yea for Mouse!

 Yes! Mouse is very brave!

 The lion picked up the mouse in its paw. This time, the mouse did not shake.

 Thank you again, Mouse. You saved my life. Can we be friends?

 Yes, Lion! Let's be friends. There are many ways that we can help each other.

 Here is one way I can help you, Mouse. I can take you where you want to go. Climb up on my back.

 Thank you, Lion!

 The lion let the mouse climb up on its back. The two friends walked off into the jungle.

What Do You Remember?

 Darken the letter by the correct answer.
Then answer the last question.

1. Why did the mouse get caught?

   Ⓐ It was running from a snake.

   Ⓑ It ran up onto the lion's back.

   Ⓒ It bit the lion's tail.

2. Why did the lion let the mouse go?

   Ⓐ The mouse was too small to eat.

   Ⓑ The lion and the mouse decided to be friends.

   Ⓒ The lion wanted to chase the monkey.

3. Why did the mouse say that it could be the lion's friend?

   Ⓐ The mouse wanted to help the lion.

   Ⓑ The mouse was lonely.

   Ⓒ The mouse wanted someone to play with.

4. The lion did not want to be friends with the mouse
   because he thought that

   Ⓐ he was the king of the jungle.

   Ⓑ a small mouse could never help a big animal like him.

   Ⓒ he did not want any friends.

5. Why did the other jungle animals not help the lion?

   Ⓐ They thought the mouse could do it alone.

   Ⓑ They thought the hunters would trap them.

   Ⓒ They thought the lion would eat them.

6. Why did the lion and the mouse become friends?

   _____

   _____

Name _____   Date _____

What's That Word?

 Read each clue. Then write the letter that matches the number to find the answer.

a	b	c	d	e	f	g	h	i	j	k	l	m
1	2	3	4	5	6	7	8	9	10	11	12	13

n	o	p	q	r	s	t	u	v	w	x	y	z
14	15	16	17	18	19	20	21	22	23	24	25	26

1. A place where lions live ____ ____ ____ ____ ____ ____
 10   21   14   7   12   5

2. Chewed ____ ____ ____ ____ ____ ____
 7   14   1   23   5   4

3. Yelled in a happy way ____ ____ ____ ____ ____ ____ ____
 3   8   5   5   18   5   4

4. The sound made by a lion ____ ____ ____ ____
 18   15   1   18

5. A problem or danger

____ ____ ____ ____ ____ ____ ____
 20   18   15   21   2   12   5

6. Having an edge that can cut easily ____ ____ ____ ____ ____
 19   8   1   18   16

Name _____   Date _____

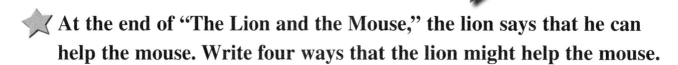

Write Away! Helping Out

⭐ At the end of "The Lion and the Mouse," the lion says that he can help the mouse. Write four ways that the lion might help the mouse.

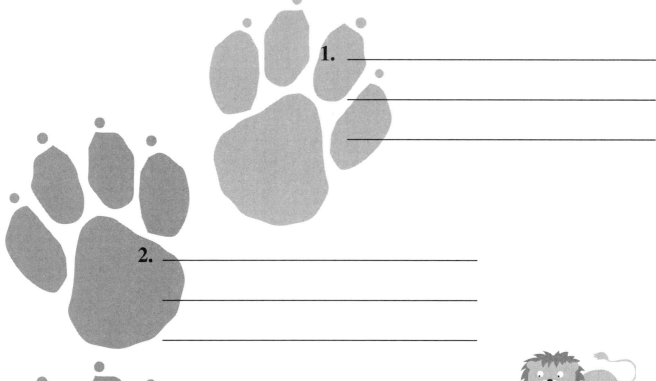

1. _____

_____

_____

2. _____

_____

_____

3. _____

_____

_____

4. _____

_____

_____

Goldilocks and the Three Bears

Play Summary

Goldilocks takes an early morning walk in the woods and enters the house of the bear family. The three bears are not home because they also took a walk while their porridge cooled. First, Goldilocks tries the porridge. She eats all the porridge in Baby Bear's bowl. Next, Goldilocks sits in the chairs and breaks Baby Bear's chair. Finally, she tries the beds and falls asleep in Baby Bear's bed. After the bears return, they discover the damage and find Goldilocks sound asleep. When Goldilocks wakes up, she screams and jumps out the window.

Meet the Players

Character	Reading Level
Narrator	1.8
Papa Bear	2.7
Mama Bear	1.8
Baby Bear	2.6
Goldilocks	2.4

Character Props

Children can use the following resources found in the back of the book to make headbands, paper-plate masks, necklaces, armbands, or puppets.
Narrator: microphone 1, p. 152
Papa Bear, p. 134
Mama Bear, p. 133
Baby Bear, p. 133
Goldilocks, p. 145

Play Props

You may wish to gather the following simple props for children to use during the play.
Table
3 bowls
3 spoons
9 chairs (6 of the chairs can be set up for beds by having 2 chairs facing each other)

Teacher's Notes

Readers' Theater for Primary Grades, SV 9309-2

Goldilocks and the Three Bears

Tapping Prior Knowledge

Before reading the play, discuss these questions with children.

1. What would you do if you found the door of a house opened?

2. How would you feel if someone broke something that belonged to you?

3. What do you think porridge is?

Vocabulary

You may wish to introduce these words prior to reading the play. Children also can practice the words using the activity master on page 49.

porridge, p. 44	*wonder*, p. 44	*pieces*, p. 45
owned, p. 44	*broke*, p. 45	*sleepy*, p. 45

Fluency: Reading with Excitement

Goldilocks and the Three Bears offers many opportunities for children to practice reading with excitement. Point out the words printed in capitals and the exclamation points. Then model how each character might say the words and sentences. Encourage all children to rehearse the parts to increase fluency.

Comprehension: Understanding Sequence

After an initial reading of the play, you may wish to draw a simple flow chart on the board and help children list the sequence of events in the play.

Extending the Play

Use these activities to enrich the children's experience with readers' theater. The activities can be completed individually, in small groups, or as a shared writing experience.

1. Have children complete any or all of the activity masters on pages 7 through 10.

2. Write a newspaper article about the break-in at the three bear's house.

3. Write a list of rules that a guest should follow when visiting.

4. Draw a picture of a favorite part in the story.

Readers' Theater

Presents

Goldilocks and the Three Bears

Cast
(in order of appearance)

Narrator _____

Papa Bear _____

Mama Bear _____

Baby Bear _____

Goldilocks _____

Long ago, a family of bears lived in a house in the woods. There was Papa Bear, Mama Bear, and Baby Bear. One morning, they found that their porridge was too hot.

 OWWW! TOO HOT!

 Yes! Yes! Too hot!

 Boo-hoo! Too hot! Too hot!

 So the three bears took a walk to wait for their porridge to cool. A little girl named Goldilocks lived near the woods. She decided to take a walk and found the small house owned by the bears.

 Look! What a cute house. It is not locked. I wonder what is inside? Look, breakfast is here. I think I'll have some.

 So Goldilocks tried each bowl of porridge. First, she tried Papa Bear's porridge.

 OWWW! Too hot!

 Then she tried Mama Bear's porridge.

 Yuck! Too cold!

 Then she tried Baby Bear's porridge.

 Yum, yum! Just right! I'll eat it all up!

 After eating Baby Bear's breakfast, Goldilocks looked around the house. She saw three chairs and wanted to try them. First, she tried Papa Bear's chair.

 Ouch! Too hard!

 Then she tried Mama Bear's chair.

 Ooof! Too soft!

 Then she tried Baby Bear's chair.

 Oh, just right! Oops! It broke!

 Goldilocks looked at the pieces of chair all around her.

 Oh, well…(yawns)…I'm so very sleepy!

45

 So Goldilocks found the bedroom. First, she got into Papa Bear's bed.

 Oh! This is too hard!

 Then she tried Mama Bear's bed.

 Oh! This is too soft!

 Then she tried Baby Bear's bed.

 Ohhh…this is snug and warm…and just right!

 Goldilocks fell fast asleep. Soon the bears came home from their walk. They were very hungry and ran to the table.

 What's this? Somebody's been eating my porridge!

 Somebody's been eating my porridge, too!

 Somebody's been eating my porridge! And it's all gone!

Page 4

 The bears began looking around their house. They found the chairs.

 Somebody's been sitting in my chair!

 Somebody's been sitting in my chair, too!

 Somebody's been sitting in my chair! And it broke!

 The bears went to their bedroom.

 Somebody's been sleeping in my bed!

 Somebody's been sleeping in my bed, too!

 Somebody's been sleeping in my bed! And there she is!

 Goldilocks woke up and saw the bears!

 EEEEEEEEK!

 She jumped out of the window and ran off. The bears never saw her again.

What Do You Remember?

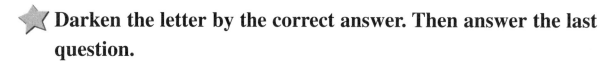 **Darken the letter by the correct answer. Then answer the last question.**

1. Where does the story take place?

   Ⓐ in Goldilock's house

   Ⓑ in a treehouse

   Ⓒ in the three bear's house

2. Why did the bears go for a walk?

   Ⓐ They went shopping.

   Ⓑ Breakfast was too hot.

   Ⓒ They went to visit friends.

3. Which porridge was too hot for Goldilocks?

   Ⓐ Papa Bear's porridge

   Ⓑ Mama Bear's porridge

   Ⓒ Baby Bear's porridge

4. What did Goldilocks do after she broke the chair?

   Ⓐ She tried the porridge.

   Ⓑ She tried the beds.

   Ⓒ She went home.

5. Where did the bears find Goldilocks?

   Ⓐ in the kitchen

   Ⓑ in the bedroom

   Ⓒ in the living room

6. Do you think that Goldilocks will go back into the woods? Why or why not?

   _____

   _____

Name _____ Date _____

What's That Word?

 Read each clue. Write a word from the box to complete the puzzle.

broke	owned	pieces	porridge	sleepy	wonder

Across

2. Belonged to a person

5. A hot breakfast food that is like oatmeal

6. Little bits

Down

1. Feeling tired

3. To want to know

4. Smashed

Name _____   Date _____

The Three Bears' Porridge

Follow the recipe to make a food that is like porridge.

You need:

1 packet of plain instant oatmeal
hot water
2 tablespoons of milk (if you would like it)
1 tablespoon of honey
jelly-like candy in the shape of bears
bowl
measuring cup
spoon

You will:

1. Pour the oatmeal into the bowl.
2. Ask an adult to help make the oatmeal.
   Follow the directions on the packet.
3. Stir the oatmeal.
4. Add the milk on the oatmeal if you want.
5. Add the honey.
6. Stir.
7. Place three bear-shaped candies on the oatmeal.
8. Enjoy!

No Problem!

Play Summary

Mrs. Smith leaves the family for several days to work in another city. Mr. Smith and the three children face the problems of trying to cook, clean, and get ready for school. The family finds out that it is really "no problem" when they learn to work together.

Meet the Players

Character	Reading Level
Narrator	3.0
Mrs. Smith	1.8
Mr. Smith	2.2
Karen	2.6
Dave	2.7
Sara	2.8

Character Props

Children can use the following resources found in the back of the book to make headbands, paper-plate masks, or paper-bag puppets.
Narrator: microphone 1, p. 152
Puppet face parts, p. 147

Play Props

You may wish to gather the following simple props for children to use during the play.
Table with four places set
1 pink sock
2 pink shirts
Paper lunch bags

Teacher's Notes

Research Base

"Readers' theater also promotes cooperative interaction with peers and makes the reading task appealing." (*Put Reading First*, p. 29)

No Problem!

Tapping Prior Knowledge

Before reading the play, discuss these questions with children.

1. What are some jobs that you do to help your family?

2. What happens if you don't do your job?

3. What do you do if your brother or sister does something that you do not like?

Vocabulary

You may wish to introduce these words prior to reading the play. Children also can practice the words using the activity master on page 59.

travel, p. 54   groaned, p. 55   special, p. 56
favorite, p. 55   dirty, p. 56   promised, p. 57

Fluency: Reading Words That Are Printed in Capital Letters

Have children turn to page 57. Point out that the last sentence is printed in all capital letters. Explain that an author will use capital letters to emphasize something important. Model how to read "NO PROBLEM!" using voice excitement and loudness. Invite children to practice reading the words together.

Comprehension: Identifying Problem and Solution

Briefly discuss the meanings of the words *problem* and *solution*. Ask children what problems the family in the story faces and record them on chart paper. Once all the problems are listed, discuss how the family solves each situation.

Extending the Play

Use these activities to enrich the children's experience with readers' theater. The activities can be completed individually, in small groups, or as a shared writing experience.

1. Have children complete any or all of the activity masters on pages 7 through 10.

2. Briefly explain the purpose of an advice column. Then have children choose one of the characters in the story. Have them write a letter asking for advice on how to solve one of the problems the character faces. Pair children and have them trade letters to write the solution, or advice, part of the letter.

3. Remind children that Karen saw an advertisement for a product that gets clothes white. Challenge children to write a jingle or draw a poster telling about the product. Encourage them to make up a name for this wonderful product.

Readers' Theater

FOR PRIMARY GRADES

Presents
No Problem!

Cast
(in order of appearance)

Narrator _____

Mrs. Smith _____

Mr. Smith _____

Karen _____

Dave _____

Sara _____

 The Smith family stood beside the taxi.

 I'm only going to be gone for ten days. We all knew that I would have to travel a little when I took this job. You all will be just fine!

 Mrs. Smith got in the car, and the taxi pulled away from the sidewalk.

 Mom is right! We will be just fine. Now go make your school lunches. I'll get the car and drive you to school.

 Mom asked me to wash some white clothes. So I need to do that right away.

 Thanks, Karen! We can dry the clothes tonight when we get home.

 Karen ran into the house. Dad went to the garage to get the car. Dave and Sara went to the kitchen and began making their lunches.

 Sara, you are only packing cookies, chips, and a box of juice. You need a sandwich and some fruit.

 I only want these snacks. I'll pack the right foods tomorrow.

No Problem!
Readers' Theater for Primary Grades, SV 9309-2

 The children heard the car horn. Dad was ready to go. Karen rushed into the kitchen and grabbed a bag of chips. Everyone got their backpacks and walked out the door. Dad sighed loudly as the children got into the car.

 That wasn't too bad for the first morning. We're only a few minutes late. I think we will have take-out for dinner.

 That night the trouble started. After dinner, Dad took the clothes out of the washing machine.

 My favorite white shirt is pink!

 Hey! My football shirt is supposed to be white. Why is it pink?

 Well, I found the problem. Karen's new red socks got washed with the white clothes.

 Everyone looked at Karen and groaned.

 Don't blame Karen. We all make mistakes. I'll try washing these clothes again to see if I can get the pink out. Now it's time for homework and then bed.

 The next four days did not go well. Mr. Smith kept forgetting to set the alarm, so everyone was late for school. Sara packed what she wanted in her lunches, and the stack of dirty dishes was growing in the sink. In fact, the whole house was a mess!

 Dad, we have five more days before Mom comes home. I'm not sure that I can eat another take-out meal.

 I need some clean white clothes, too. I can't wear pink socks to gym.

 I guess we need a plan. We need to work together.

 I can do a little cooking. I'll fix the meals for the rest of the time. I'll even wash the dishes.

 I saw an ad about a special soap that makes clothes snowy white. I'll try washing the clothes in it. Also, I'll make the school lunches the night before. Maybe we will leave on time then.

 That will be good for Sara. She's been taking junk food.

 I want to help, too. I'll set Dad's alarm clock every night.

 And I'll clean the house. We just need to work together.

 No problem!

 The next five days went quickly. Everyone did the jobs they promised. If something did happen, everyone helped.

 Sara, you left your lunch in the house.

 I'll go get it. No problem!

 The dog got his muddy paws on the floor.

 I'll clean it up. No problem!

 After ten days, Mrs. Smith returned. She thought she was in the wrong house.

 Wow! Look how clean the house is. And dinner is on the table. I'm really surprised! I was afraid to tell you that I will be leaving again next week.

 Dad and the children looked at each other and laughed…

 NO PROBLEM!

What Do You Remember?

 Darken the letter by the correct answer. Then answer the last question.

1. Why did Mrs. Smith leave for several days?
   - Ⓐ She went to visit her mother.
   - Ⓑ She went on a work trip.
   - Ⓒ She went to the hospital.

2. What happened to the white clothes?
   - Ⓐ Karen forgot to wash them.
   - Ⓑ They got too small.
   - Ⓒ They turned pink.

3. Why do you think the house was messy?
   - Ⓐ No one wanted to do the work.
   - Ⓑ The house was being painted.
   - Ⓒ Water spilled out from the washing machine.

4. What did Sara do to help?
   - Ⓐ She cleaned up after the dog.
   - Ⓑ She washed the dishes.
   - Ⓒ She set the alarm clock.

5. How did Mrs. Smith feel when she got back home?
   - Ⓐ angry
   - Ⓑ surprised
   - Ⓒ sad

6. Do you think the Smith family will work together when Mrs. Smith leaves again? Why or why not?

   _____

   _____

Name _____   Date _____

What's That Word?

 Read each clue. Write a word from the box to complete each sentence.

| dirty   favorite   groaned   promised   special   travel |

1. Sara likes to _____ on airplanes.

2. After eating, we took the _____ dishes to the sink.

3. Juan _____ to do his homework before going to the park.

4. My _____ football team won four games in a row.

5. Isa _____ when she saw the muddy footprints on the clean floor.

6. Mom made a _____ cake for Lee's birthday.

Name _____ Date _____

Write Away! No Problem Cooking

 Suppose you had to cook dinner. What would you make? Write the recipe. Draw a picture of the food on a plate.

You need:

_____ _____

_____ _____

_____ _____

_____ _____

You will:

_____

_____

_____

_____

_____

Readers' Theater for Primary Grades, SV 9309-2

The Strongest One of All

Play Summary

Mr. and Mrs. Mouse think it is time for their daughter to marry. They decide that their daughter should marry the strongest one in the land. The family visits many suitors in their quest, but finds out that the little mouse living under a statue is really the strongest one of all.

Meet the Players

Character	Reading Level
Narrator	3.2
Mr. Mouse	2.8
Mrs. Mouse	1.8
Daughter mouse	2.0
Mr. Sun	2.4
Mr. Cloud	1.9
Mr. Wind	2.9
Mr. Statue	1.7
Suitor mouse	1.5

Character Props

Children can use the following resources found in the back of the book to make headbands, paper-plate masks, necklaces, armbands, or paper-bag puppets.
Narrator: microphone 1, p. 152
Mr. Mouse, p. 141
Mrs. Mouse, p. 142
Daughter mouse, Girl mouse, p. 141
Mr. Sun, p. 157
Mr. Cloud, p. 149
Mr. Wind, p. 158
Mr. Statue, p. 157
Suitor mouse, Boy mouse, p. 140

Play Props

You may wish to gather the following simple props for children to use during the play.
Sky backdrop
Town backdrop

Teacher's Notes

The Strongest One of All

Tapping Prior Knowledge

Before reading the play, discuss these questions with children.

1. What can you do that shows how strong you are?

2. What are some ways that people and animals show how strong they are?

3. Does *strong* always mean how much you can lift? What are some other meanings for the word *strong*?

Vocabulary

You may wish to introduce these words prior to reading the play. Children also can practice the words using the activity master on page 69.

daughter, p. 65	*kind*, p. 65	*strong*, p. 65
beautiful, p. 65	*smart*, p. 65	*front*, p. 66

Fluency: Reading Questions

The Strongest One of All offers many opportunities for children to practice reading questions. Have children turn to page 65. Point out the question marks and explain that the voice rises at the end of a question. Read a questioning sentence with a flat voice and then as it should be read. Have children discuss which sounds better. Invite partners to take turns reading questions in the play to practice this fluency skill.

Comprehension: Recognizing a Folktale

Explain that all folktales have the same characteristics, including animals that talk, repetitive actions, and the teaching of a lesson. Explore how *The Strongest One of All* is an example of a folktale.

Extending the Play

Use these activities to enrich the children's experience with readers' theater. The activities can be completed individually, in small groups, or as a shared writing experience.

1. Have children complete any or all of the activity masters on pages 7 through 10.

2. Remind children that the words *beautiful*, *kind*, and *smart* are used to describe the daughter. Then draw a web with the three words in the outside circles, and invite children to add other words that could be used to describe the daughter. Next, ask children to choose another character in the story. Have them draw a web and write words to describe that character.

3. Challenge children to write a folktale with the title *The Smartest One of All.*

Readers' Theater

FOR PRIMARY GRADES

Presents

The Strongest One of All

Readers' Theater

Cast
(in order of appearance)

Narrator _____

Mr. Mouse _____

Mrs. Mouse _____

Daughter Mouse _____

Mr. Sun _____

Mr. Cloud _____

Mr. Wind _____

Mr. Statue _____

Suitor Mouse _____

 There once was a family of mice who lived in a field. The mother and father were very proud of their daughter. She was beautiful, kind, and smart.

 Our daughter should get married. Who do you suggest?

 It must be someone who is beautiful, kind, and smart like our daughter.

 There are many who are beautiful, kind, and smart. Our daughter should marry someone who is very special.

 That is true. Who would you like to marry, daughter? Who do you think is special?

 I would like to marry someone who is strong. There is much work to do around a house.

 That is it! Our daughter will marry the strongest one in the land.

 I think our daughter should marry Mr. Sun. He is the strongest one of all.

 And so, Mr. and Mrs. Mouse went to find Mr. Sun.

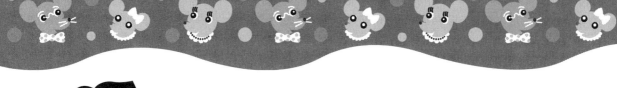

 Mr. Sun, you are the strongest one of all.
Will you marry our daughter?

 I am not the strongest one of all. Ask Mr. Cloud.
He can make me go away any time he wants by
moving in front of me.

 And so, Mr. and Mrs. Mouse went to find
Mr. Cloud.

 Mr. Cloud, you are the strongest one of all.
Will you marry our daughter?

 I am not the strongest one of all. Ask Mr. Wind.
He can blow me away any time he wants.

 And so, Mr. and Mrs. Mouse went to find
Mr. Wind.

 Mr. Wind, you are the strongest one of all.
Will you marry our daughter?

 I am not the strongest one of all. Ask Mr. Statue
in the town square. As hard as I blow, I can't
make him move.

 And so, Mr. and Mrs. Mouse went to find
Mr. Statue.

The Strongest One of All
Readers' Theater for Primary Grades, SV 9309-2

 Mr. Statue, you are the strongest one of all. Will you marry our daughter?

 I am not the strongest one of all. Ask the mouse who lives under my feet. The deeper he digs, the more I tip over. The mouse is really the strongest one of all.

 And so, Mr. and Mrs. Mouse went home to get their daughter. The family went back to the town square.

 Oh, Mouse, you are the strongest one of all. Will you marry me?

 Yes, I am the strongest one of all. I will marry you!

 And so, Mr. and Mrs. Mouse were happy. Their daughter was happy, too. They had finally found the strongest one of all.

Name _____   Date _____

What Do You Remember?

 Darken the letter by the correct answer. Then answer the last question.

1. Whom did the mice want their daughter to marry?

    Ⓐ the most beautiful one of all

    Ⓑ the smartest one of all

    Ⓒ the strongest one of all

2. Who did Mr. Sun say was the strongest?

    Ⓐ Mr. Statue

    Ⓑ Mr. Cloud

    Ⓒ Mr. Wind

3. Why was Mr. Wind stronger than Mr. Cloud in the story?

    Ⓐ The wind could make the cloud move.

    Ⓑ The wind could make the cloud hold still.

    Ⓒ The wind could make the cloud change shape.

4. Who did the mice visit after seeing Mr. Wind?

    Ⓐ Mr. Statue

    Ⓑ Mr. Sun

    Ⓒ the mouse

5. How did the little mouse make the statue fall?

    Ⓐ He ate the statue.

    Ⓑ He moved dirt from under the statue.

    Ⓒ He pushed it over.

6. Do you think the little mouse is the strongest one of all? Why or why not?

    _____

    _____

Readers' Theater for Primary Grades, SV 9309-2

What's That Word?

 Write a word from the box that means the opposite. Then circle the word in the puzzle.

beautiful	daughter	front	kind	smart	strong

1. weak _____

2. back _____

3. ugly _____

4. mean _____

5. dumb _____

6. son _____

```
s  v  i  m  r  s  p  o  l  e
m  b  e  a  u  t  i  f  u  l
a  d  y  s  g  r  a  r  k  i
r  o  n  h  g  o  w  o  e  f
t  a  u  k  i  n  d  n  j  k
b  t  d  a  u  g  h  t  e  r
y  w  o  p  l  f  n  z  d  s
```

Name _____   Date _____

Write Away! The Strongest One of All Contest

⭐ Suppose there is a contest to find the strongest one of all. Who do you think should win? Write sentences telling who you think should win and why. (Remember, "strong" has many meanings.) Then draw a picture of the person.

_____

_____

_____

_____

_____

_____

_____

_____

Chicken Little

Play Summary

Chicken Little is looking for grain when an acorn falls on her head. She thinks that the sky is falling and runs to tell the king. Along the way, Chicken Little meets friends, including a fox who tries to trick the group.

Meet the Players

Character	Reading Level
Narrator	2.4
Chicken Little	1.3
Cocky Locky	1.1
Goosey Loosey	1.1
Ducky Lucky	1.9
Turkey Lurkey	2.7
Foxy Loxy	1.8

Character Props

Children can use the following resources found in the back of the book to make headbands, paper-plate masks, necklaces, vests, armbands, or paper-bag puppets.
Narrator: microphone 1, p. 152
Chicken Little, p. 135
Cocky Locky, p. 143
Goosey Loosey, p. 138
Ducky Lucky, p. 137
Turkey Lurkey, p. 144
Foxy Loxy, p. 138

Play Props

You may wish to gather the following simple props for children to use during the play.
Tree backdrop
Castle backdrop
Chairs for a fox den
Umbrella

Teacher's Notes

Research Base

"For some children, a readers' theater event could provide a rare opportunity for the less-skilled reader to be on equal footing with better readers." (Rinehart, p. 85)

Chicken Little

Tapping Prior Knowledge

Before reading the play, discuss these questions with children.

1. Has anything ever fallen from above and hit you? Tell what happened.

2. How did you feel?

3. What could fall and make someone think the sky was falling?

Vocabulary

You may wish to introduce these words prior to reading the play. Children also can practice the words using the activity master on page 81.

young, p. 75	*sly*, p. 78	*problem*, p. 78	*howling*, p. 79
grain, p. 75	*watching*, p. 78	*den*, p. 78	*searched*, p. 79

Fluency: Reading Phrases in a Series Separated by Commas

Chicken Little offers many opportunities for children to practice reading phrases and commas. Have children turn to page 77 and find the words spoken by the narrator. Point out that commas separate the character names that are in a list. Explain that the comma signals a brief pause. Then model reading the sentence at the appropriate speed. Read the sentence again as if there are no commas. Have children discuss which is easier to understand. Invite partners to take turns reading the sentence to develop fluency.

Comprehension: Recognizing a Character

Lead children in a discussion of common traits animal characters have in folktales. For example, challenge children to name stories that have a fox. Guide children to understand that the fox usually appears tricky, or sly. Continue by looking at characteristics common to hens (perseverance), wolves (mean), rabbits (playfully tricky), etc.

Extending the Play

Use these activities to enrich the children's experience with readers' theater. The activities can be completed individually, in small groups, or as a shared writing experience.

1. Have children complete any or all of the activity masters on pages 7 through 10.

2. Have children write a script that tells what happens when Chicken Little and her friends meet with the king.

3. Have children create a map to show where each part of the play occurs, beginning with the place where the acorn falls on Chicken Little and ending at the king's castle.

Readers' Theater FOR PRIMARY GRADES

Presents

Chicken Little

Readers' Theater
FOR PRIMARY GRADES

Cast
(in order of appearance)

Narrator _____

Chicken Little _____

Cocky Locky _____

Goosey Loosey _____

Ducky Lucky _____

Turkey Lurkey _____

Foxy Loxy _____

Chicken Little
Readers' Theater for Primary Grades, SV 9309-2

 Page 1

 Once there was a young hen named Chicken Little. One day Chicken Little was looking for grain, and an acorn fell and hit her on the head.

 Oh, my! Oh, my! The sky is falling! The sky is falling! I must go and tell the king.

 So she set off to see the king. Soon she met her friend Cocky Locky.

 Where are you going, Chicken Little?

 Oh, Cocky Locky! A piece of the sky fell and hit me on the head! The sky is falling! I must go and tell the king!

 Oh, no! May I go with you to tell the king?

 Yes, yes! But we must run!

 So Chicken Little and Cocky Locky set off to see the king. Soon they met their friend Goosey Loosey.

Chicken Little
Readers' Theater for Primary Grades, SV 9309-2

 Where are you going, Chicken Little and Cocky Locky?

 A piece of the sky fell and hit me on the head!

  The sky is falling! We must go and tell the king!

 Oh, no! May I go with you to tell the king?

  Yes, yes! But we must run!

 So Chicken Little, Cocky Locky, and Goosey Loosey set off to tell the king. Soon they met their friend Ducky Lucky.

 Where are you going, Chicken Little, Cocky Locky, and Goosey Loosey?

 A piece of the sky fell and hit me on the head!

 The sky is falling! We must go and tell the king!

 Oh, no! May I go with you to tell the king?

 Yes, yes! But we must run!

So Chicken Little, Cocky Locky, Goosey Loosey, and Ducky Lucky set off to tell the king. Soon they met their friend Turkey Lurkey.

 Where are you going, Chicken Little, Cocky Locky, Goosey Loosey, and Ducky Lucky?

 A piece of the sky fell and hit me on the head!

 The sky is falling! We must go and tell the king!

 **Page 4**

 Oh, no! May I go with you to tell the king?

 Yes, yes! But we must run!

 A sly fox was watching as the friends set off down the road. He stopped them just as they were running past.

 Hello, my friends. Where are you going on such a fine day?

 A piece of the sky fell and hit me on the head!

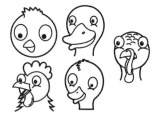 The sky is falling! We must go and tell the king!

 Well, that is a problem, but I can help you. Come this way. If you go right through my den, there is a door on the other side. It will lead you right to the king's castle.

Page 5

 The fox began to smack his lips, ready for lunch as the four friends walked into his den. Just then, the sound of barking and howling dogs filled the air. BARK! BARK! HOWL! HOWL!

 Oh, no! It's a fox hunt! The dogs have found my trail. HELP! HELP!

 So Foxy Loxy ran away as fast as he could. Chicken Little and her friends met with the king. The king gave Chicken Little an umbrella. She could use it when she searched for acorns. Now when the sky falls, Chicken Little doesn't even feel it. And all the friends lived happily ever after.

What Do You Remember?

 Darken the letter by the correct answer. Then answer the last question.

1. What fell on Chicken Little's head?
   Ⓐ grain
   Ⓑ an acorn
   Ⓒ a leaf

2. Why did Foxy Loxy show Chicken Little and her friends the fastest way to see the king?
   Ⓐ He was going to eat them.
   Ⓑ He wanted to help them.
   Ⓒ He wanted to feed them lunch.

3. Why did Foxy Loxy run away?
   Ⓐ Turkey Lurkey pecked him.
   Ⓑ Dogs were chasing him.
   Ⓒ The king made him leave.

4. What did the king give to Chicken Little?
   Ⓐ an umbrella
   Ⓑ a medal
   Ⓒ a nest

5. What is this play mostly about?
   Ⓐ things falling out of the sky
   Ⓑ silly animals that act without thinking
   Ⓒ the life of a fox

6. Why do you think Chicken Little wanted to tell the king about the sky falling?

   _____

   _____

Name _____   Date _____

What's That Word?

 Read each clue. Write a word from the box on the lines.

| den   grain   problem   searched   sly   watching   young |

1. Looked for a long time __ __ __ __ __ ☐ __ __
  1

2. Something that is wrong __ __ ☐ __ __ __ __
  2

3. Seeing ☐ __ __ __ __ __ __
  3

4. Tricky __ ☐ __
  4

5. Seeds from wheat __ __ __ ☐ __
  5

6. Home for a fox __ __ ☐
  6

7. Not old __ __ __ __ ☐
  7

 Write the letters in the boxes above in order to answer the question.

What noise made Foxy Loxy run away?

__ __ __ __ __ __ __
1 2 3 4 5 6 7

Chicken Little
Readers' Theater for Primary Grades, SV 9309-2

Name _____ Date _____

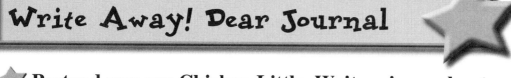

Write Away! Dear Journal

⭐ Pretend you are Chicken Little. Write a journal entry telling about the events that happened during the day.

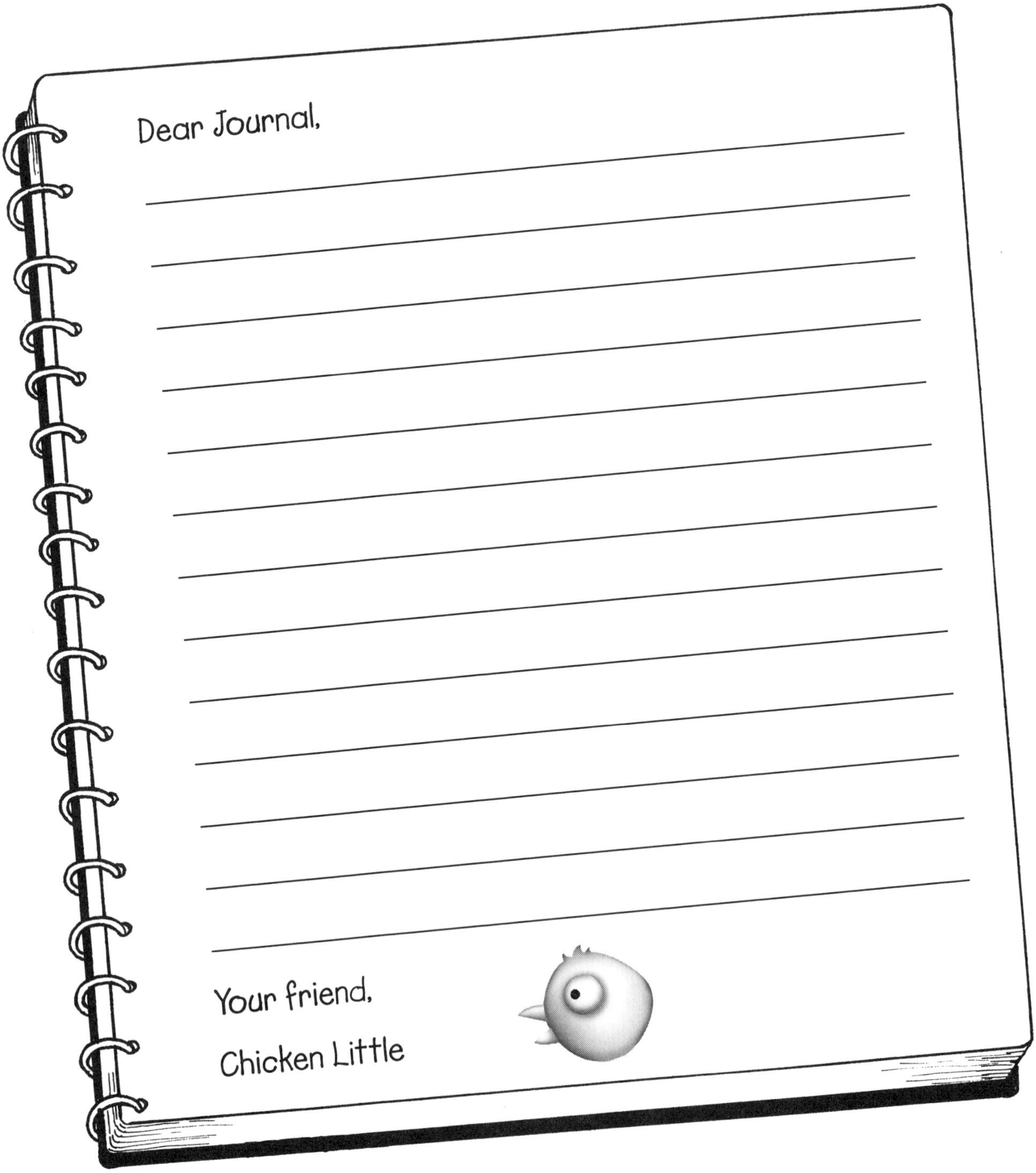

Dear Journal,

_____

_____

_____

_____

_____

_____

_____

_____

_____

_____

Your friend,

Chicken Little

The Planets

Play Summary

This rhyming play identifies the most important features of each planet in our solar system.

Meet the Players

Character	Reading Level
Narrator 1	3.3
Narrator 2	3.5
Mercury	2.4
Venus	2.7
Earth	3.0
Mars	3.2
Jupiter	3.4
Saturn	3.9
Uranus	3.0
Neptune	2.9
Pluto	2.2

Character Props

Children can use the following resources found in the back of the book to make necklaces, vests, badges, armbands, or stick puppets.
Narrator 1: microphone 1, p. 152
Narrator 2: microphone 2, p. 152
Mercury, p. 153
Venus, p. 153
Earth, p. 153
Mars, p. 153
Jupiter, p. 154
Saturn, p. 155
Uranus, p. 156
Neptune, p. 156
Pluto, p. 155

Play Props

You may wish to gather the following simple props for children to use during the play.
Outer space backdrop

The Planets

Tapping Prior Knowledge

Before reading the play, discuss these questions with children.

1. On which planet do we live?

2. What are the names of the other eight planets?

3. What do you know about any of the planets?

Vocabulary

You may wish to introduce these words prior to reading the play. Children also can practice the words using the activity master on page 91.

asteroids, p. 87   *solid*, p. 88   *gassy*, p. 88   *telescope*, p. 89
desert, p. 88   *endlessly*, p. 88   *colorful*, p. 88   *explore*, p. 89

Fluency: Reading Rhyming Text

The Planets offers many opportunities for children to practice reading rhyming text. Turn to page 88 and read the passage about Mars. Help children notice words that rhyme. Point out that the sentences form couplets with an AABB pattern. Finally, point out that rhyming words may have different spelling patterns (*four/core*). You may wish to point out that some words may not rhyme exactly but have the same vowel sound (for example, in Jupiter: *five/sky*). Invite partners to choose the planet that they find interesting and rehearse the passage to develop fluency.

Comprehension: Recognizing Facts

Have children turn to page 88 and read aloud the information about Earth. Point out that the four lines give several facts about our planet. Have children identify these facts and write their responses on the board. Next, assign partners one of the other eight planets. Have them draw a picture of the planet and record the facts identified in the selection on the back of the drawing. Ask partners to share their work with the class.

Extending the Play

Use these activities to enrich the children's experience with readers' theater. The activities can be completed individually, in small groups, or as a shared writing experience.

1. Have children complete any or all of the activity masters on pages 7 through 10.

2. Challenge groups of children to draw a mural showing the solar system.

3. Have children research a planet and find additional facts. Ask children to draw, cut out, and color the back and front of the planet. Then have them write the facts on cards and attach them to string to hang from the planet like a mobile.

Readers' Theater

FOR PRIMARY GRADES

Presents

The Planets

Cast
(in order of appearance)

Narrator 1 _____

Narrator 2 _____

Mercury _____

Venus _____

Cast, page 2
(in order of appearance)

Earth _____

Mars _____

Jupiter _____

Saturn _____

Uranus _____

Neptune _____

Pluto _____

The solar system's one big place,
Filled with things all over space.
But at the center of this world
Is the sun, I'm sure you've learned.
Countless stars light up the sky,
While comets and asteroids fly right by.

Yes, the solar system's one big place,
Filled with things all over space.
Our solar system's not complete
Without nine planets, which you'll meet.
Here they are to share with you
How they look and what they do.

I am Mercury. I'm planet one.
I'm the closest to the sun.
I'm the fastest of the nine
And the hottest all the time.

I am Venus. I'm planet two.
From Earth, I look like a star to you.
When you see the sky at night,
Clouds around me reflect sunlight.

 I am Earth. I'm planet three.
Plants and animals live on me.
From rocky mountains to desert sand,
People play and work the land.

 I am Mars. I'm planet four.
I am solid to the core.
I am covered in a deep red sand
And look just like a desert land.

 I am Jupiter. I'm planet five.
I'm the largest in the sky.
A large, red spot is found on me.
It's a storm that blows endlessly.

 I am Saturn. I'm planet six.
I'm mostly made of a gassy mix.
I have many colorful rings.
They're made from dust and icy things.

 I am Uranus. I'm planet seven.
I spin on my side again and again.
Lots of clouds gather around me.
And scientists think I might have a sea.

Readers' Theater for Primary Grades, SV 9309-2

I am Neptune. I'm planet eight.
I have the fastest winds to date.
With a telescope, I look blue.
I'm a very cold planet, too.

I am Pluto. I'm planet nine.
I am the last one in the line.
I'm the coldest one of all.
I'm also the smallest planet ball.

You met the planets here today
And heard about their special ways.
There still is much for us to know
About the planets and where they go.

It could be YOU that will explore
Our solar system to find out more.
The solar system's one big place,
Filled with things all over space.

What Do You Remember?

 Darken the letter by the correct answer. Then answer the last question.

1. Why is Earth different from every other planet?
   - Ⓐ It has a desert.
   - Ⓑ It has water.
   - Ⓒ It has life.

2. Why is Mercury the hottest planet?
   - Ⓐ It is the closest to the sun.
   - Ⓑ It is made of hot gas.
   - Ⓒ It has red sand.

3. Which planet is the farthest from the sun?
   - Ⓐ Pluto
   - Ⓑ Neptune
   - Ⓒ Venus

4. Which planet spins on its side?
   - Ⓐ Earth
   - Ⓑ Jupiter
   - Ⓒ Uranus

5. What is Saturn known for?
   - Ⓐ a red spot
   - Ⓑ colorful rings
   - Ⓒ fast winds

6. Which planet would you like to visit? Why?

   _____

   _____

What's That Word?

 Read each clue. Write a word from the box to complete the puzzle.

asteroids	colorful	desert	endlessly
explore	gassy	solid	telescope

Across

2. Never ending

3. A tool that is used to see things far away

5. Something that is hard and has a shape

6. Full of color

7. Not solid

8. Land that has very little growing or living on it

Down

1. Large rocks that circle around the sun

4. To go to a new place and learn about it

Name _____ Date _____

Write Away! Take a Trip

⭐ Create a travel poster to visit one of the planets. Describe what people will see, do, and discover. Plan your poster below. When the plan is done, use it to make a larger poster to hang in the classroom.

The Planets
Readers' Theater for Primary Grades, SV 9309-2

The Clouds

Play Summary

Best friends Juan and Linda spend an afternoon watching clouds. They see shapes in the clouds and make up stories about what they see. Their fun comes to an end when a storm blows in. They race to safety just as the thunderstorm arrives.

Meet the Players

Character	Reading Level
Narrator 1	2.4
Narrator 2	2.7
Juan	2.8
Linda	2.1

Character Props

Children can use the following resources found in the back of the book to make paper-bag puppets, paper-plate masks, or stick puppets.
Narrator 1: microphone 1, p. 152
Narrator 2: microphone 2, p. 152
Puppet face parts, p. 147

Play Props

You may wish to gather the following simple props for children to use during the play.
Sky backdrop
Clouds in the following shapes: king with a crown, a town, a tower, two flowers, a cat, a bear, dark storm clouds
Soundtrack of storm sounds

Research Base

"Readers' theater potentially offers exposure, support, and practice so that even beginning readers can read at higher levels of fluency on targeted text." (Rinehart, p. 85)

Teacher's Notes

The Clouds

Tapping Prior Knowledge

Before reading the play, discuss these questions with children.

1. Have you ever played a game in which you find shapes in clouds? Tell me about it.

2. How do clouds look on a bright, sunny day?

3. How do clouds look before it begins to storm?

Vocabulary

You may wish to introduce these words prior to reading the play. Children also can practice the words using the activity master on page 100.

amazed, p. 96	*noticed*, p. 97	*frown*, p. 97	*lightning*, p. 97
fluffy, p. 96	*sneaking*, p. 97	*thunder*, p. 97	*spark*, p. 97

Fluency: Reading with Excitement

The Clouds offers many opportunities for children to practice reading with excitement. Have children turn to page 98. Point out the word printed in capitals and the exclamation points. Discuss how Juan might be feeling at this point in the play. Then model how Juan might say these sentences. Encourage all children to rehearse the parts to increase fluency.

Comprehension: Identifying Sequence

Write the numbers *1* through *6* on chart paper. Invite children to retell the most important parts of the story in their own words. Add more numbers if needed. Review the list using time-order words. Reread the story to make sure the events are listed in order.

Extending the Play

Use these activities to enrich the children's experience with readers' theater. The activities can be completed individually, in small groups, or as a shared writing experience.

1. Have children complete any or all of the activity masters on pages 7 through 10.

2. Invite children to view clouds and write their own story about what they see happening as the clouds change.

3. Provide several days of newspaper weather reports. Also show taped examples of weather segments from local television stations. Invite children to write their own weather reports to share with the class. Provide mural paper so they can draw maps.

Readers' Theater

FOR PRIMARY GRADES

Presents
The Clouds

Cast
(in order of appearance)

Narrator 1 _____

Narrator 2 _____

Juan _____

Linda _____

 Juan and Linda are the best of friends.
They play most every day.
They might just sit and watch TV,
Or go to the park to play.

 This Saturday they are outside,
Sitting under a tree.
Juan and Linda watch the sky.
They're amazed at what they see.

 Look at all those fluffy clouds!
They're really racing fast.

 I think I see some different shapes
As they're floating past.

 I think you're right, for there I see
A king with a big crown.
But now it's changing to a shape
That looks like a small town.

 That town is changing shape again!
It looks like a tall tower.
The wind is blowing it in two,
So now I see some flowers.

 As the hours slowly passed,
Juan and Linda had great fun.
But they never noticed that the clouds
Blocked out the shining sun.

 Look, I see a little cat!
And there I see a bear.
It's sneaking up behind the cat
To give it such a scare.

 Over there I see a cow
Playing with a clown.
But the sky looks like it's changing.
The clouds are turning brown.

 The clouds don't look too happy.
The clown's begun to frown.
It's bumping into other clouds.
I hear a thunder sound!

 Come on, Juan! It's time to go!
The clouds are really dark.
Pretty soon I think we'll see
A flash of lightning spark!

 The friends ran quickly down the street.
They raced to Linda's door.
Along the way the thunder boomed.
The wind began to roar.

 WHEW! We made it just in time!
We're safe from that big storm!

 Let's go inside before it rains,
So we can then get warm.

 It was fun to look at clouds
Before the thundershower.

 We'll have to do it once again,
But at another hour.

What Do You Remember?

 Darken the letter by the correct answer. Then answer the last question.

1. At the beginning of the play, what is the day like?

Ⓐ sunny

Ⓑ stormy

Ⓒ foggy

2. Why do the clouds keep changing shapes?

Ⓐ Lightning pulls them apart.

Ⓑ The wind blows them.

Ⓒ Juan and Linda look at them from different sides.

3. What does the word "sneaking" mean?

Ⓐ moving happily

Ⓑ moving loudly

Ⓒ moving quietly

4. What was the first sign that a storm was coming?

Ⓐ Juan and Linda heard thunder.

Ⓑ It began to rain.

Ⓒ The clouds turned brown.

5. What sound did the wind make?

Ⓐ a boom

Ⓑ a roar

Ⓒ a crash

6. Do you think that Juan and Linda will watch the clouds again?
Tell why you think as you do.

_____

_____

Name _____   Date _____

What's That Word?

 Write a word from the box to complete each sentence.

amazed	fluffy	frown	lightning
noticed	sneaking	spark	thunder

1. Lee _____ the dark clouds in the sky.

2. "Where did the white, _____ clouds go?" she wondered.

3. "These dark clouds are _____ quietly over the sun," she said.

4. Lee was _____ at how quickly the sky changed.

5. She was not happy and began to _____.

6. Lee heard _____ far away.

7. Then she saw a bright _____ of light in the sky.

8. "That was a flash of _____!" Lee said.

Name _____ Date _____

Write Away! Cloud Story

 Look at the clouds below. What shapes do you see? Name them. Then write a story about one of the cloud shapes on the back of this page.

_____

_____

_____

_____

The Clouds
Readers' Theater for Primary Grades, SV 9309-2

Name _____   Date _____

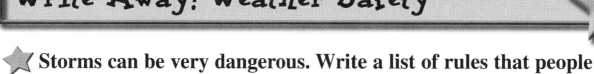

Write Away! Weather Safety

⭐ **Storms can be very dangerous. Write a list of rules that people should follow during a storm.**

_____

_____

_____

_____

_____

_____

_____

_____

_____

_____

_____

_____

The Gingerbread Boy

Play Summary

A little old woman and a little old man bake a gingerbread boy that comes to life. He runs away from the people and many animals. The gingerbread boy stops at a river, where he meets a fox. The fox slyly offers to take the gingerbread boy across the river, at which time the fox eats the cookie.

Meet the Players

Character	Reading Level
Narrator	1.8
Old woman	1.7
Old man	2.2
Gingerbread boy	1.6
Cow	2.0
Duck	2.1
Horse	2.1
Sheep	3.2
Fox	1.8

Character Props

Children can use the following resources found in the back of the book to make headbands, paper-plate masks, armbands, puppets, or necklaces.
Narrator: microphone 1, p. 152
Old woman, p. 146
Old man, p. 146
Gingerbread boy, p. 151
Cow, p. 135
Duck, p. 137
Horse, p. 139
Sheep, p. 143
Fox, p. 138

Play Props

You may wish to gather the following simple props for children to use during the play.
Bowl
Spoon
House backdrop
Blue mural paper for river

The Gingerbread Boy

Tapping Prior Knowledge

Before reading the play, discuss these questions with children.

1. What is gingerbread?

2. What are some things you must do when you make cookies?

3. If a cookie became real, how do you think it would feel about being eaten?

Vocabulary

You may wish to introduce these words prior to reading the play. Children also can practice the words using the activity master on page 113.

lonely, p. 107   *real*, p. 108   *tasty*, p. 109   *delicious*, p. 109
dough, p. 107   *chase*, p. 108   *crunchy*, p. 109   *dessert*, p. 110

Fluency: Reading Ellipses and Dashes

The Gingerbread Boy offers many opportunities for children to practice reading ellipses and dashes. Have children turn to page 111. Point out the ellipses and the dashes. Explain that these punctuation marks mean that a reader should briefly pause. Then model how the gingerbread boy and the fox might say these sentences. Assign partners the part of the fox and gingerbread boy and allow time for them to practice reading fluently. After a while, have them switch roles.

Comprehension: Making Inferences

Point out that the story never tells us why the gingerbread boy runs away, and we must look at information in the story and think of facts we know to help us find out why. Help children conclude that the cookie runs away because he thinks he will be eaten.

Extending the Play

Use these activities to enrich the children's experience with readers' theater. The activities can be completed individually, in small groups, or as a shared writing experience.

1. Have children complete any or all of the activity masters on pages 7 through 10.

2. Have children create a poster that tells about a missing gingerbread boy.

3. Review the story and have children find all the adjectives used to describe the gingerbread boy. Draw a web with the title "gingerbread" and write the adjectives in the outer circles. Then ask children to create a web using a food they do not like. Have them include adjectives describing the food in the outer circles. Encourage them to write a paragraph about the food using the adjectives in their web.

4. Ask children to draw a picture of a gingerbread boy they would like to make. Then make the gingerbread cookie recipe on page 114. Have children duplicate the cookie as close to the picture as they can.

Teacher's Notes

Presents

The Gingerbread Boy

Readers' Theater

FOR PRIMARY GRADES

Cast
(in order of appearance)

Narrator _____

Old Woman _____

Old Man _____

Gingerbread Boy _____

Cow _____

Duck _____

Horse _____

Sheep _____

Fox _____

Readers' Theater for Primary Grades, SV 9309-2

 Once upon a time, a little old woman and a little old man lived in a little house in the woods. They were lonely, for they had no children.

 I wish we had a little boy or a little girl. It would be wonderful to have a child to love.

 If we had a child, we could play games, too.

 Well, we may not have children, but I can bake a make-believe child. I will make a gingerbread boy! We can hold him and talk to him.

 What a good idea! I will help you.

 So the little old woman mixed up the dough and shaped it into a boy. The little old man added eyes, a nose, and a mouth. They popped the gingerbread boy into the oven. After a while, the wonderful smell of gingerbread filled the house.

 Our gingerbread boy must be done. How nice it will be to have him here!

 Okay, boy, we are opening the oven. Come meet us!

 When the little old woman and the little old man opened the oven door, out jumped the gingerbread boy.

 Hello, old woman! Hello, old man! I'm the gingerbread boy!

 What is this! Our gingerbread boy is real!

 What a wonderful surprise!

 Just as the old woman started to pick up the gingerbread boy, he said…

 Run, run! You can't catch me!
I'm out of here—just watch and see!

 Stop! Stop!

 And she began to chase him. The gingerbread boy ran past the little old man.

 Stop! Stop!

 Run, run! You can't catch me!
I'm out of here—just watch and see!

Page 3

The gingerbread boy kept running. He ran past a cow.

Moo, moo! Stop! Stop! You look very tasty. I would like to eat you!

Run, run! You can't catch me! I'm out of here—just watch and see!

And the cow began to chase him. The gingerbread boy kept running. He ran past a duck.

Quack, quack! Stop! Stop! You are brown and crunchy. I would like to eat you!

Run, run! You can't catch me! I'm out of here—just watch and see!

And the duck began to chase him. The gingerbread boy kept running. He ran past a horse.

Neigh, neigh! Stop! Stop! You smell delicious. I would like to eat you!

Run, run! You can't catch me! I'm out of here—just watch and see!

Readers' Theater for Primary Grades, SV 9309-2

 And the horse began to chase him. The gingerbread boy kept running. He ran past a sheep.

 Baa, baa! Stop! Stop! I haven't eaten dessert yet. I would like to eat you!

 Run, run! You can't catch me! I'm out of here—just watch and see!

 And the sheep began to chase him. The gingerbread boy kept running. Soon he came to a river. He saw a fox standing by the river.

 Hello, gingerbread boy, where are you going in such a hurry?

 I've run away from a little old woman, a little old man, a cow, a duck, a horse, a sheep…and I can run away from you!

 Oh, I am sure you can because I can see that you are a very smart gingerbread boy! But I can help you. Quick, here they come! Jump on my tail, and I can take you to the other side of the river. Then they'll never catch you!

 Well-l-l-l…okay.

 So the gingerbread boy hopped onto the tail of the fox.

 Gingerbread boy—the water is getting deeper. Jump on my back so that you won't get wet!

 Well-l-l-l…okay.

 Gingerbread boy—the water is getting deeper. Jump on my head so that you won't get wet!

 Well-l-l-l…okay.

 Gingerbread boy, it is very deep now. Jump on my nose so that you won't get wet!

 Suddenly, the fox lifts his nose. The gingerbread boy flies into the air. SNAP!

 MMMMMMMM, delicious! That was a great way to end lunch.

 And that was the end of the gingerbread boy!

Name _____   Date _____

What Do You Remember?

 Darken the letter by the correct answer. Then answer the last question.

1. Why did the little old woman want to bake a gingerbread boy?
   Ⓐ She was hungry.
   Ⓑ She was happy.
   Ⓒ She was lonely.

2. Why were the people surprised when they opened the oven?
   Ⓐ The gingerbread boy was real.
   Ⓑ The gingerbread boy was crunchy.
   Ⓒ The gingerbread boy was gone.

3. Why did the gingerbread boy run?
   Ⓐ He wanted to get exercise.
   Ⓑ It was hot in the oven.
   Ⓒ He did not want to be eaten.

4. Why did the gingerbread boy stop at the river?
   Ⓐ He could not get across.
   Ⓑ He wanted to talk to the fox.
   Ⓒ He decided to go back home.

5. Why did the gingerbread boy climb on the nose of the fox?
   Ⓐ He wanted to see where he was going.
   Ⓑ He did not want to get wet.
   Ⓒ He could use the nose as a diving board.

6. What happened to the gingerbread boy? How do you know?

_____

_____

Name _____   Date _____

What's That Word?

 Read each clue. Write a word from the box on the lines.

chase	crunchy	delicious	dough
lonely	real	tasty	

1. A mixture of flour, sugar, and eggs that is baked ☐ __ __ __ __
   1

2. Not make-believe __ ☐ __ __
   2

3. To run after __ __ __ ☐ __
   3

4. Very good to eat __ __ __ __ __ __ __ __ ☐
   4

5. Feeling alone __ __ __ ☐ __ __
   5

6. Noisy when eaten __ ☐ __ __ __ __ __
   6

7. Full of taste __ __ __ ☐ __
   7

 Write the letters in the boxes above in order to answer the question.

What was the gingerbread boy?

__ __ __ __ __ __ __
1 2 3 4 5 6 7

Name _____   Date _____

Gingerbread Boy Cookies

 Follow the recipe to make gingerbread boy cookies.

You need:

1 egg

$\frac{1}{2}$ cup shortening

$\frac{1}{2}$ cup brown sugar

$1\frac{1}{2}$ cup flour

1 package butterscotch instant
   pudding

$1\frac{1}{2}$ teaspoons ginger

$\frac{1}{2}$ teaspoon cinnamon

$\frac{1}{2}$ teaspoon baking soda

1 can frosting

candies, raisins, sprinkles

bowls

measuring cup

spoon

rolling pin

gingerbread boy cookie cutter

cookie trays

pancake turner

You will:

1. Mix egg, shortening, and brown sugar.
2. Stir in remaining ingredients.
3. Roll out dough and cut with the cookie cutter.
4. Bake for 10 minutes at 350°F.
5. Decorate the cookies.
6. Enjoy!

The Around the World Lunch

Play Summary

Pepito's aunt packs a special lunch just for Pepito. Inside the lunch bag is a special Cuban sandwich. Pepito wonders what the sandwich will taste like as his friends describe foods from around the world that their family members cook for them.

Meet the Players

Character	Reading Level
Narrator	3.2
Aunt Lena	2.0
Pepito	3.1
Gina	1.7
Lee	2.5
Tara	3.3
Ray	3.1
Ana	3.4

Character Props

Children can use the following resources found in the back of the book to make necklaces, vests, badges, armbands, or stick puppets.
Narrator: microphone 1, p. 152
Puppet face parts, p. 147
Ham and cheese submarine sandwich, p. 149
Peanut butter and honey sandwich, p. 150
Won tons, p. 150
Plantains, p. 150
Poori, p. 150
Buñuelos, p. 149

Play Props

You may wish to gather the following simple props for children to use during the play.
Lunch bag
Posters of map outlines: Cuba, Mexico, Africa, India, China
Large table
6 chairs

Teacher's Notes

The Around the World Lunch

Tapping Prior Knowledge

Before reading the play, discuss these questions with children.

1. What are some foods that are special in your family?

2. What kinds of foods do you pack in a school lunch?

3. What do you think a Cuban sandwich might taste like?

Vocabulary

You may wish to introduce these words prior to reading the play. Children also can practice the words using the activity master on page 123.

sandwich, p. 119   won tons, p. 120   poori, p. 120
honey, p. 120   plantains, p. 120   buñuelos, p. 121

Fluency: Reading Questions

The Around the World Lunch offers many opportunities for children to practice reading questions. Have children turn to page 121. Point out the question marks and remind children that the voice rises at the end of a question. Read a questioning sentence with a flat voice and then as it should be read. Have children discuss which sounds better. Invite partners to take turns practicing the fluency skill of reading questions.

Comprehension: Making Predictions

Review the play with children. Ask them to notice how the children in the play make predictions about what the Cuban sandwich might taste like. Ask children if they thought about what the sandwich might taste like when they read the play. Have children tell if they were surprised to learn how the Cuban sandwich tasted.

Extending the Play

Use these activities to enrich the children's experience with readers' theater. The activities can be completed individually, in small groups, or as a shared writing experience.

1. Have children complete any or all of the activity masters on pages 7 through 10.

2. Using a world map, help children find the countries named in the play.

3. Review proper nutrition. Then have children plan a nutritious lunch menu.

4. Bring to class a variety of breads from around the world for children to sample. Have children choose two breads to compare and contrast in a Venn diagram.

Readers' Theater

FOR PRIMARY GRADES

Presents

The Around the World Lunch

Pepito

Readers' Theater

Cast
(in order of appearance)

Narrator _____

Aunt Lena _____

Pepito _____

Gina _____

Lee _____

Tara _____

Ray _____

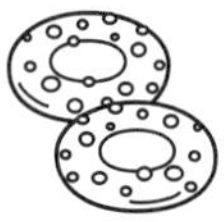

Ana _____

 Pepito's aunt was in town for a visit. She had packed Pepito's lunch for school.

 I made a surprise for your school lunch. It is a Cuban sandwich. I put it in your lunch. Don't look inside the bag until it is time to eat lunch!

 What is a Cuban sandwich, Aunt Lena?

 You will have to wait until lunch to find out! Remember, it is a surprise.

 I love sandwiches, and I love surprises. I can't wait until lunch. Thank you, Aunt Lena!

 Pepito was very excited. He hurried out the door to school. When Pepito got to school, he told all of his friends about the surprise food.

 My aunt made a Cuban sandwich for lunch. I wonder what it tastes like.

 Gina began to talk.

www.harcourtschoolsupply.com
© Harcourt Achieve Inc. All rights reserved.

119

The Around the World Lunch
Readers' Theater for Primary Grades, SV 9309-2

 Sometimes my grandmother visits me. She makes a special sandwich for me, too. She makes a peanut butter and honey sandwich.

 Lee began to talk.

 Sometimes my grandfather cooks for me. He makes food from China. I like it when he makes won tons. Won tons are like stuffed dumplings.

 Tara began to talk.

 My aunt cooks for me, too. She makes plantains to go with my lunch. It is a food from Africa. A plantain tastes like a fried banana. It's sweet and mushy.

 Ray began to talk.

My dad cooks foods from India all the time. He cooks poori to go with my lunch. He taught me how to cook poori. It is like fried bread.

 Ana began to talk.

 My mom cooks buñuelos to go with my lunch. Buñuelos are a food from Mexico. They taste like flat, crunchy doughnuts. I love to eat buñuelos!

 Everyone was curious about the special Cuban sandwich that Pepito had in his lunch bag. Finally, the noon bell rang. Pepito and his friends walked quickly to the lunchroom. Pepito pulled the Cuban sandwich out of the bag.

 Well, here is the sandwich! It doesn't look like there is anything unusual on it.

 Well, Pepito, take a bite!

 What does your sandwich taste like?

 Does it taste like crunchy doughnuts?

 Does it taste like sweet and mushy bananas?

 Is it good?

 MMMMMM, I know what it tastes like. It tastes just like a ham and cheese sandwich!

What Do You Remember?

 Darken the letter by the correct answer. Then answer the last question.

1. Who packed Pepito's lunch?
   - Ⓐ Pepito's friend
   - Ⓑ Pepito's aunt
   - Ⓒ Pepito's mother

2. Why couldn't Pepito look in the bag?
   - Ⓐ The teacher would not let him.
   - Ⓑ The lunch smelled funny.
   - Ⓒ The lunch was a surprise.

3. From what country do plantains come?
   - Ⓐ Africa
   - Ⓑ Mexico
   - Ⓒ India

4. What did a Cuban sandwich taste like?
   - Ⓐ bananas
   - Ⓑ peanut butter
   - Ⓒ ham and cheese

5. How did Pepito feel about his sandwich when he ate it?
   - Ⓐ He didn't like it.
   - Ⓑ He thought it tasted good.
   - Ⓒ He wanted to trade it.

6. Of all the food talked about in this play, which one would you like to eat? Why?

_____

_____

What's That Word?

 Read each food name. Draw a line to the matching picture.

1. poori

a.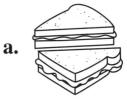

2. plantains

b.

3. sandwich

c.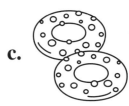

4. won tons

d.

5. buñuelos

e.

6. honey

f.

Name _____ Date _____

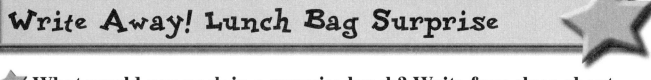

Write Away! Lunch Bag Surprise

⭐ **What would you pack in a surprise lunch? Write four clues about the food on the bag below. Then draw a picture of the food on the back of the paper. Trade clues with a classmate. Can he or she guess the surprise food?**

1. _____
   _____
   _____

2. _____
   _____
   _____

3. _____
   _____
   _____

4. _____
   _____
   _____

A Sheep in the Peppers

Play Summary

A sheep gets into a garden and begins to eat the beautiful peppers. A girl and other animals try to convince the sheep to leave. Finally, a bee stings the sheep to encourage it to go away.

Meet the Players

Character	Reading Level
Girl	2.0
Sheep	2.5
Rooster	3.4
Dog	3.0
Cow	2.8
Bee	2.6

Character Props

Children can use the following resources found in the back of the book to make headbands, vests, necklaces, armbands, or puppets.
Puppet face parts, p. 147 (or Goldilocks, p. 145)
Sheep, p. 143
Rooster, p. 143
Dog, p. 136
Cow, p. 135
Bee, p. 134

Play Props

You may wish to gather the following simple props for children to use during the play.
Plant
Garden backdrop

Research Base

"One of the unique contributions of readers' theater... is that it offers an integrated language event with an authentic communication purpose. These students were excited about reading their scripts because they *could* and because someone wanted to listen." (Rinehart, p. 87)

A Sheep in the Peppers

Tapping Prior Knowledge

Before reading the play, discuss these questions with children.

1. Suppose an animal got into your garden and started to eat the plants. How would you feel?

2. What could you do to get the animal out of the garden?

3. Do you think that a bee could help get the animal out of the garden? How?

Vocabulary

You may wish to introduce these words prior to reading the play. Children also can practice the words using the activity master on page 131.

plenty, p. 128   *peck*, p. 128   *stubborn*, p. 129
speak, p. 128   *regret*, p. 129   *flee*, p. 129

Fluency: Reading Onomatopoeia Words

Invite children to make sounds like animals. Write the sounds as words. Explain that authors sometimes use sound words to help create interest in a play or story. Have children turn to page 128. Ask children how a rooster might read the words *cock-a-doodle-doo*!

Comprehension: Understanding Cause and Effect

Discuss examples of cause and effect, such as: *The wind blew and made the door close.* Invite children to share other cause and effect examples. Then have children find the effects of the following two story events: *The sheep likes peppers.* and *The bee says it will sting the sheep.*

Extending the Play

Use these activities to enrich the children's experience with readers' theater. The activities can be completed individually, in small groups, or as a shared writing experience.

1. Have children complete any or all of the activity masters on pages 7 through 10.

2. Have children plan a garden and the plants they would like to grow in it. Have them draw a map of their garden on mural paper.

3. Have children retell the story from the viewpoint of the sheep.

4. Help children compile a list of animals and the sounds they make.

Readers' Theater

FOR PRIMARY GRADES

Presents
A Sheep in the Peppers

Cast
(in order of appearance)

Girl _____

Sheep _____

Rooster _____

Dog _____

Cow _____

Bee _____

127

 **Page 1**

 I grow pretty peppers.
Pretty peppers do I grow.
Plenty of pretty peppers,
In plenty of pretty rows.

 Bah, bah, bah, bah!
Chomp, chomp, chomp, chomp!

 Mr. Sheep, don't eat my peppers!
Please get out of here.
I'll have no peppers left to sell;
That is my biggest fear!

 Peppers are a tasty treat.
Peppers are what I want to eat!

 Cock-a-doodle-doo, cock-a-doodle-doo!
Don't eat those peppers! Hear me speak.
Or I will peck you with my beak!

 Peppers are a tasty treat.
Peppers are what I want to eat!

 Woof, woof, woof, woof!
Get away, Mr. Sheep, let them be,
Or you will have to deal with me!

A Sheep in the Peppers
Readers' Theater for Primary Grades, SV 9309-2

 Peppers are a tasty treat.
Peppers are what I want to eat!

 Moo, moo, moo, moo!
Go on now, just get away,
Or you will regret this day!

 Peppers are a tasty treat.
Peppers are what I want to eat!

 Buzz, buzz, buzz, buzz!
You did not listen, you stubborn thing.
Now I will get you with my sting!

 Ouch! Ouch! You hurt me, Bee!
Now it's time for me to flee!
While peppers are a tasty treat,
I no longer want them to eat.

 Oh, thank you, Bee!
You saved the day.
You made that sheep run far away.

What Do You Remember?

 Darken the letter by the correct answer. Then answer the last question.

1. What is this play mostly about?

   Ⓐ animals that are mean

   Ⓑ a girl who is trying to catch a sheep

   Ⓒ a sheep that likes to eat peppers

2. Why does the girl grow the peppers?

   Ⓐ so that she can sell them

   Ⓑ so that she can eat them

   Ⓒ so that she can make spices with them

3. What might the dog do to get the sheep out of the garden?

   Ⓐ peck the sheep

   Ⓑ bite the sheep

   Ⓒ lick the sheep

4. What does "stubborn" mean?

   Ⓐ very funny

   Ⓑ not easily moved

   Ⓒ well liked

5. Who made the sheep leave the garden?

   Ⓐ a cow

   Ⓑ a rooster

   Ⓒ a bee

6. Why do you think that the sheep no longer wanted to eat peppers?

   _____

   _____

Name _____   Date _____

What's That Word?

 Read the clue. Then write the letter that matches the number to find the answer.

a	b	c	d	e	f	g
1	2	3	4	5	6	7
h	i	j	k	l	m	n
8	9	10	11	12	13	14
o	p	q	r	s	t	u
15	16	17	18	19	20	21
v	w	x	y	z		
22	23	24	25	26		

1. To talk ___ ___ ___ ___ ___
           19   16   5   1   11

2. More than enough ___ ___ ___ ___ ___ ___
           16   12   5   14   20   25

3. To run away quickly ___ ___ ___ ___
           6   12   5   5

4. To feel sorry ___ ___ ___ ___ ___ ___
           18   5   7   18   5   20

5. To strike with the beak ___ ___ ___ ___
           16   5   3   11

6. Not easily moved ___ ___ ___ ___ ___ ___ ___ ___
           19   20   21   2   2   15   18   14

Name _____ Date _____

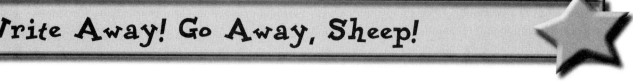
Write Away! Go Away, Sheep!

⭐ Think about another animal that might help get the hungry sheep out of the garden. Write another part to the play. Try to use the same rhyme and rhythm pattern of the play. Then draw a picture of the animal and the sheep.

_____

_____

_____

A Sheep in the Peppers
Readers' Theater for Primary Grades, SV 9309-2

Baby Bear

Mama Bear

Props: Animals
Readers' Theater for Primary Grades, SV 9309-2

Papa Bear

Bee

Props: Animals
Readers' Theater for Primary Grades, SV 9309-2

Chicken

Cow

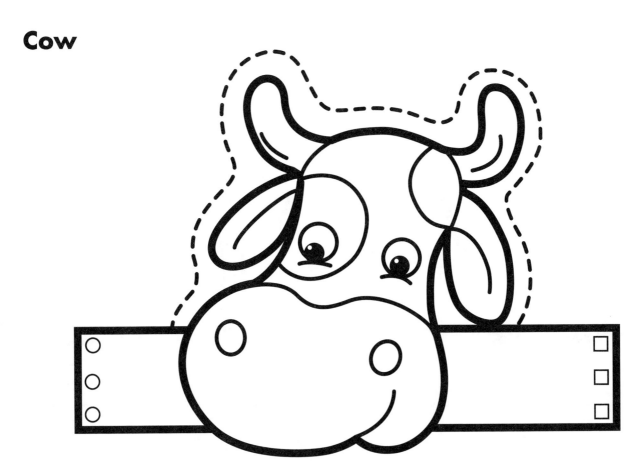

Props: Animals
Readers' Theater for Primary Grades, SV 9309-2

Crab

Dog

Props: Animals
Readers' Theater for Primary Grades, SV 9309-2

Duck

Fish

Props: Animals
Readers' Theater for Primary Grades, SV 9309-2

Fox

Goose

Props: Animals
Readers' Theater for Primary Grades, SV 9309-2

Horse

Lion

Props: Animals
Readers' Theater for Primary Grades, SV 9309-2

Monkey

Boy Mouse

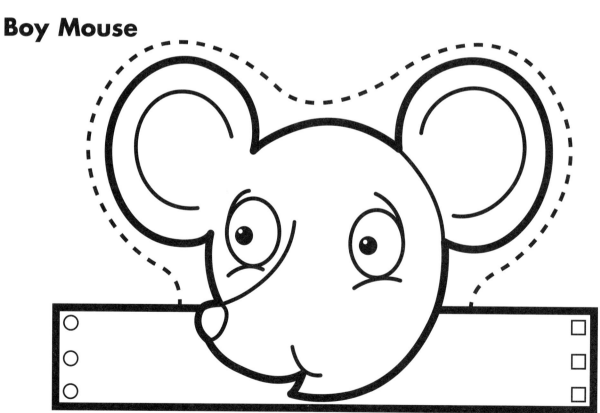

Props: Animals
Readers' Theater for Primary Grades, SV 9309-2

Girl Mouse

Mr. Mouse

Props: Animals
Readers' Theater for Primary Grades, SV 9309-2

Mrs. Mouse

Pig

Props: Animals
Readers' Theater for Primary Grades, SV 9309-2

Rooster

Sheep

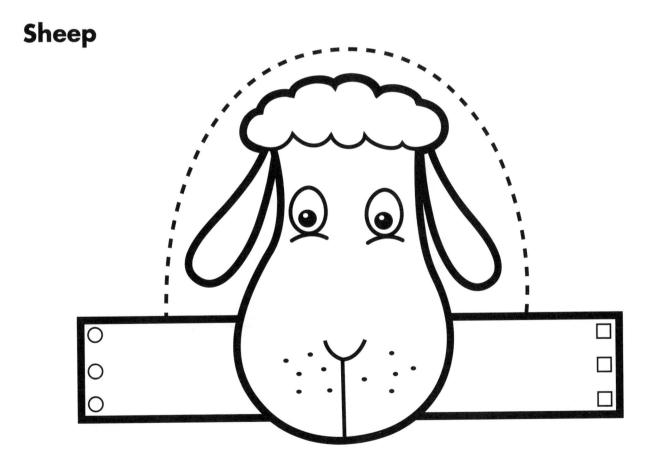

Props: Animals
Readers' Theater for Primary Grades, SV 9309-2

Snake

Turkey

Props: Animals
Readers' Theater for Primary Grades, SV 9309-2

Turtle

Goldilocks

Props: Animals/People
Readers' Theater for Primary Grades, SV 9309-2

Old Man

Old Woman

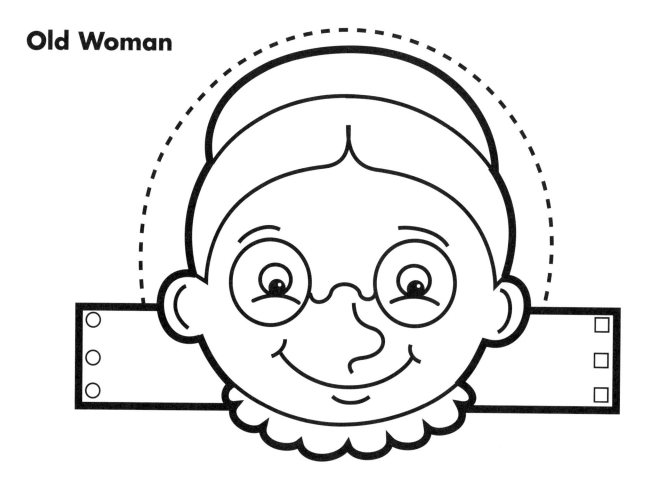

Readers' Theater for Primary Grades, SV 9309-2

Puppet Face Parts

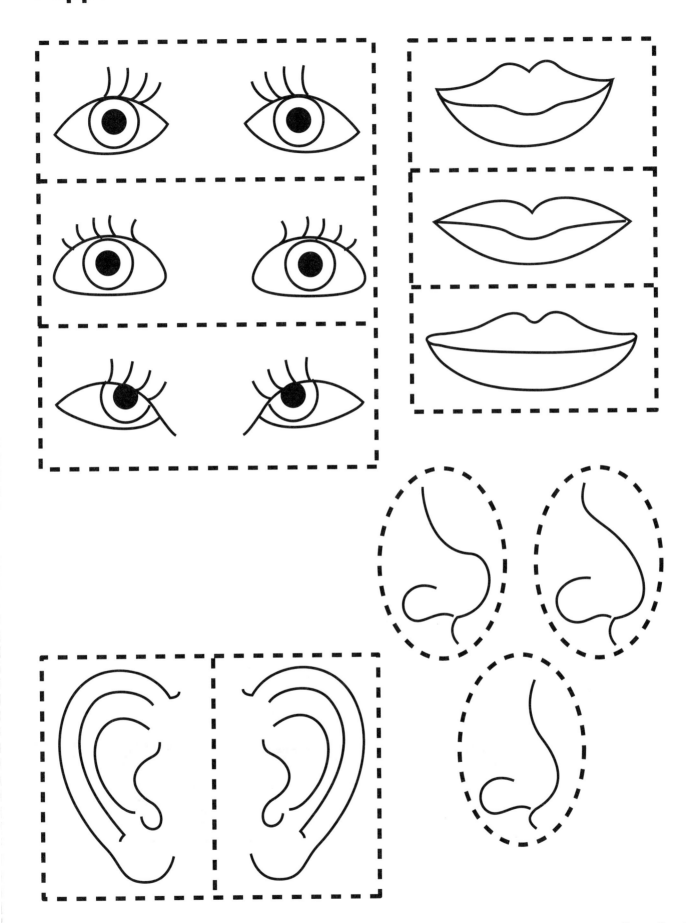

Badge

Bag of Money

Bus

Props: Things
Readers' Theater for Primary Grades, SV 9309-2

Chalkboard

Cloud

Buñuelos

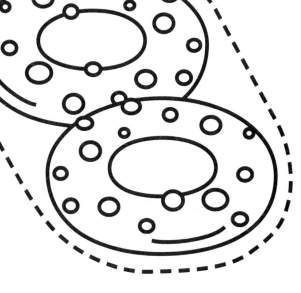

**Ham and Cheese
Submarine Sandwich**

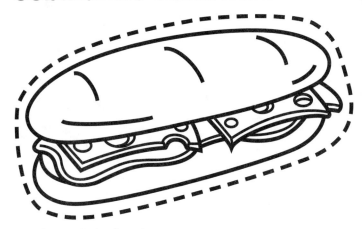

Props: Things
Readers' Theater for Primary Grades, SV 9309-2

Peanut Butter and Honey Sandwich

Plantains

Poori

Won Tons

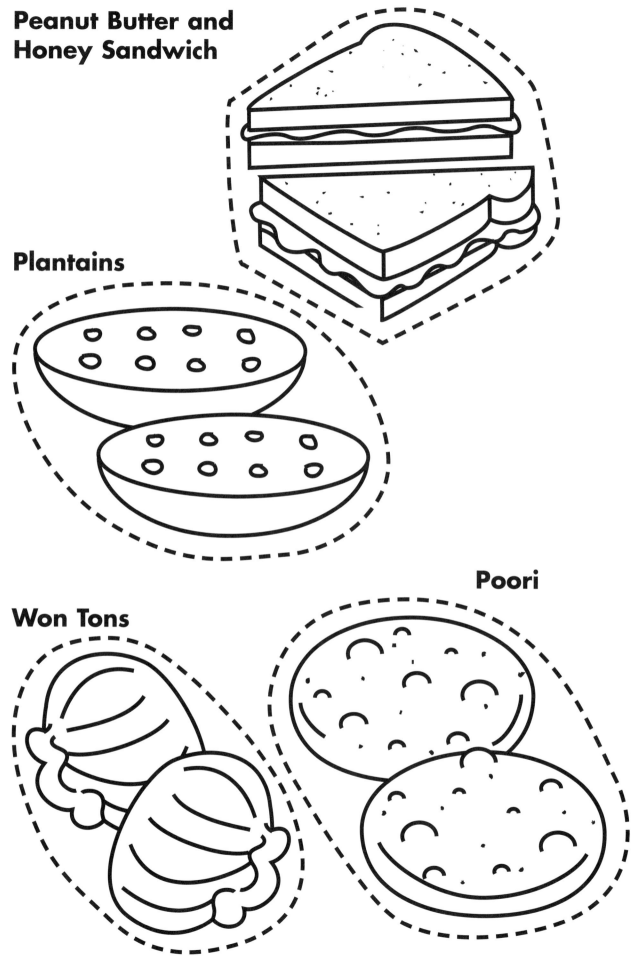

Props: Things
Readers' Theater for Primary Grades, SV 9309-2

Gingerbread Boy

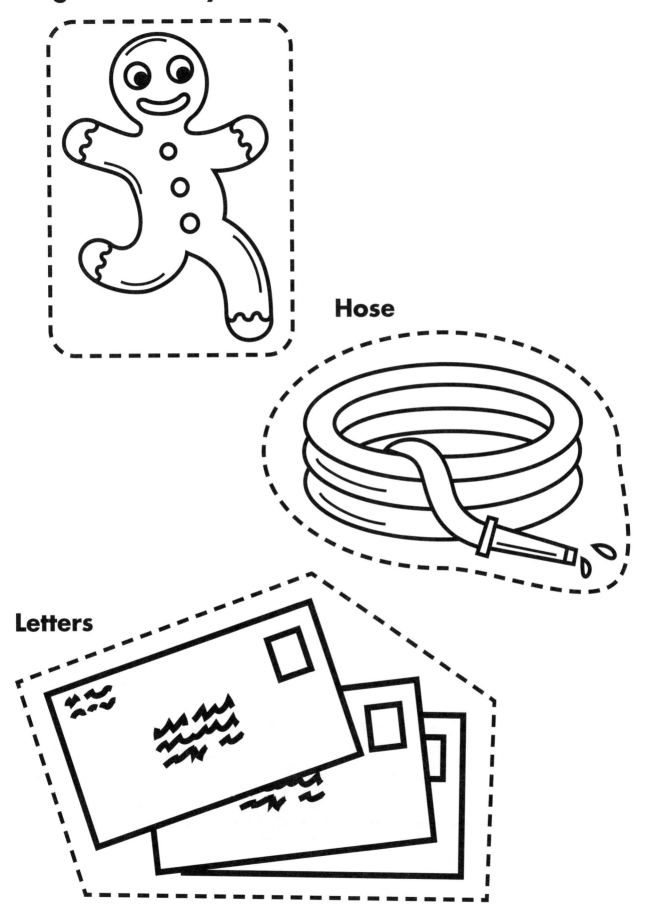

Hose

Letters

Microphone 1

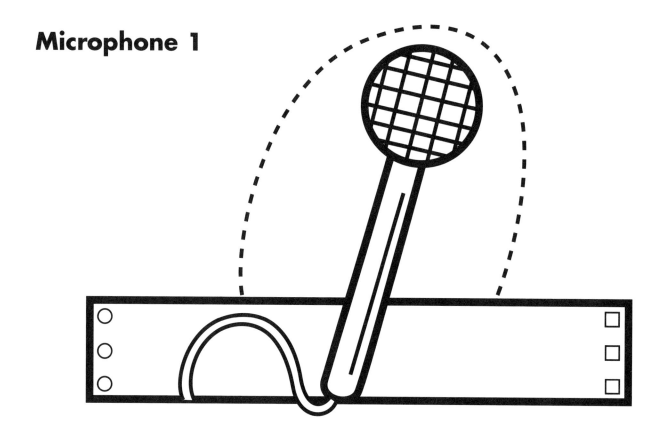

Microphone 2

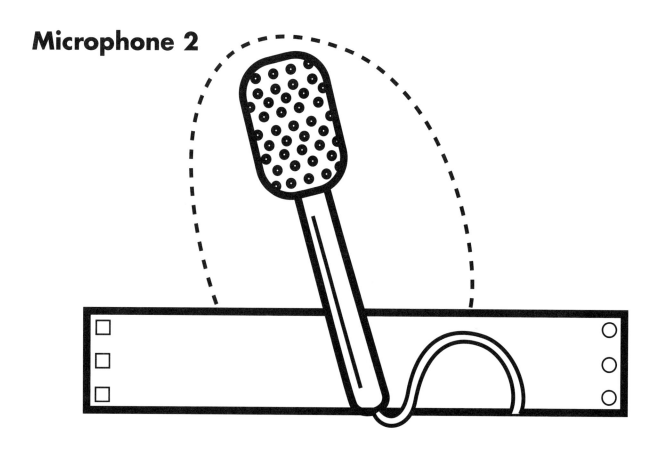

Mercury

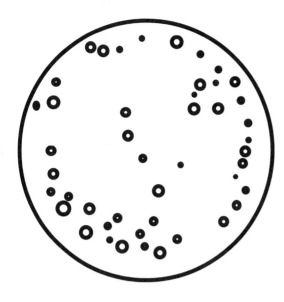

Venus

Earth

Mars

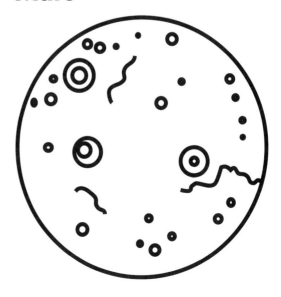

Jupiter

Saturn

Pluto

Props: Things

Readers' Theater for Primary Grades, SV 9309-2

Uranus

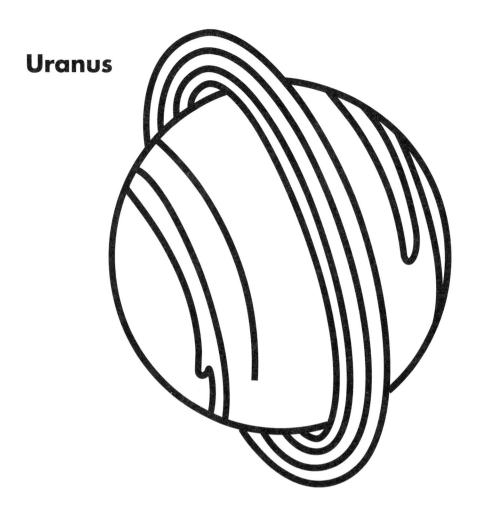

Neptune

Readers' Theater for Primary Grades, SV 9309-2

Statue

Stethoscope

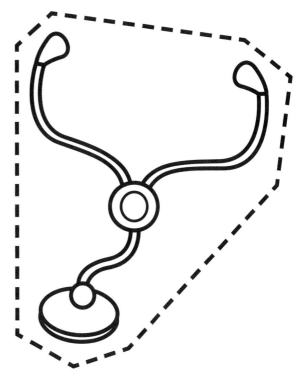

Sun

Props: Things
Readers' Theater for Primary Grades, SV 9309-2

Toothbrush

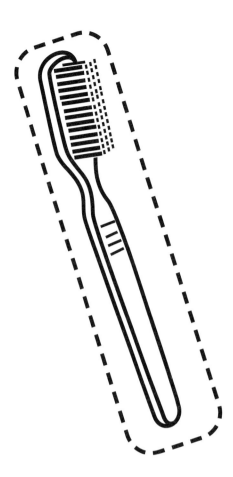

Wind

Props: Things
Readers' Theater for Primary Grades, SV 9309-2

Readers' Theater for Primary Grades

Answer Key

Page 16
1. A   2. B   3. C
4. B   5. A
6. The story is about working together to do a job.

Page 17
1. string   2. kind   3. large
4. stone   5. shore

Page 28
1. C   2. A   3. A
4. B   5. C
6. Be sure children note that people in a community have many needs and that it takes the jobs and skills of many different people to meet those needs.

Page 29
1. hose   2. dough
3. uniform   4. address
5. protect   6. teeth
7. cough   8. chalk
9. price   10. badge

Page 38
1. B   2. A   3. A
4. B   5. C
6. The mouse shows that it cared for the lion by helping him.

Page 39
1. jungle   2. gnawed   3. cheered
4. roar   5. trouble   6. sharp

Page 48
1. C   2. B   3. A
4. B   5. B
6. Mostly likely answer: Goldilocks will not go back because she was scared.

Page 49

Across	Down
2. owned	1. sleepy
5. porridge	3. wonder
6. pieces	4. broke

Page 58
1. B   2. C   3. A
4. C   5. B
6. Most likely answer: The Smith family will work together because they found out it is easier to work together to get jobs done.

Page 59
1. travel   2. dirty   3. promised
4. favorite   5. groaned   6. special

Page 68
1. C   2. B   3. A
4. A   5. B   6. Answers will vary.

Page 69
1. strong   2. front   3. beautiful
4. kind   5. smart   6. daughter

s	v	i	m	r	s	p	o	l	e
m	b	e	a	u	t	i	f	u	l
a	d	y	s	g	r	a	r	k	i
r	o	n	h	g	o	w	o	e	f
t	a	u	k	i	n	d	n	l	k
b	t	d	a	u	g	h	t	e	r
y	w	o	p	l	f	n	z	d	s

Page 80
1. B   2. A   3. B
4. A   5. B   6. Answers will vary.

Readers' Theater for Primary Grades

Answer Key

Page 81
1. searched   2. problem   3. watching
4. sly   5. grain   6. den
7. young
Answer: howling

Page 90
1. C   2. A   3. A
4. C   5. B   6. Answers will vary.

Page 91

Across	Down
2. endlessly	1. asteroids
3. telescope	4. explore
5. solid	
6. colorful	
7. gassy	
8. desert	

Page 99
1. A   2. B   3. C
4. C   5. B
6. Most likely answer: Yes, they will watch the clouds again. They had fun watching the clouds, and they spent most of the day playing the game.

Page 100
1. noticed   2. fluffy
3. sneaking   4. amazed
5. frown   6. thunder
7. spark   8. lightning

Page 101
Most likely answers: skate, tree, train, flower

Page 112
1. C   2. A   3. C
4. A   5. B
6. The fox ate the gingerbread boy. The cookie was on the fox's nose. When the fox lifted his nose, the boy flew into the air, and the fox ate him. The fox said that he was a good dessert.

Page 113
1. dough   2. real   3. chase
4. delicious   5. lonely   6. crunchy
7. tasty
Answer: dessert

Page 122
1. B   2. C   3. A
4. C   5. B   6. Answers will vary.

Page 123
1. b   2. e   3. a
4. f   5. c   6. d

Page 130
1. C   2. A   3. B
4. B   5. C
6. Most likely answer: The sheep was afraid that he would be stung again.

Page 131
1. speak   2. plenty   3. flee
4. regret   5. peck   6. stubborn

References

Armbruster, B.B., Lehr, F., & Osborn, J. (2001). *Put reading first: The research building blocks for teaching children to read.* Washington, D.C.: National Institute for Literacy.

Rinehart, S.D. (1999). "Don't think for a minute that I'm getting up there": Opportunities for readers' theater in a tutorial for children with reading problems. *Journal of Reading Psychology, 20,* 71–89.